2

how to be a great
working
Mum

how to be a great working Mum

tracey godridge
and martine gallie

foulsham

LONDON • NEW YORK • TORONTO • SYDNEY

foulsham

The Publishing House, Bennetts Close, Cippenham, Slough, Berkshire, SL1 5AP, England

Foulsham books can be found in all good bookshops and direct from www.foulsham.com

ISBN: 978-0-572-03419-1

Copyright © 2008 W. Foulsham & Co. Ltd

Cover photograph © Superstock

A CIP record for this book is available from the British Library

The moral right of the authors has been asserted

Northamptonshire Libraries & Information Services NW

Askews

Neither the editors of W. Foulsham & Co. Ltd nor the authors nor the publisher take responsibility for any possible consequences from any treatment, procedure, test, exercise, action or application of medication or preparation by any person reading or following the information in this book.

While every effort has been made to ensure the accuracy of all the information contained within this book, neither the authors nor the publisher can be liable for any errors. In particular, since laws change from time to time, it is vital that each individual checks relevant legal details for themselves.

Printed in Great Britain by Creative Print and Design (Wales), Ebbw Vale

Contents

Introduction

Today more mums work than ever before. Current research shows that around 70 per cent of mums have either a part-time or full-time job. For many, work is about having enough money to put food on the table, pay the mortgage or take the family on holiday once a year. For others, especially mums who've trained hard to get where they are, work is about their own self-esteem and independence. For lots of us it's a combination of all these factors, plus a few others, too – like having a life outside the home, forging friendships, being part of a team, having a sense of direction and discovering new opportunities.

Whatever your reasons for being a working mum, you are going to need a huge amount of guts and determination. Guts because however much you love your job and trust your childcarer, there will always be that niggle at the back of your mind that perhaps you should be at home full time with your child. Determination because, realistically, there will be times when the stress of juggling the school-run alongside work deadlines barely leaves you with enough energy to get undressed before collapsing into bed at the end of the day.

Part of the problem, of course, is that you care. You want to be a great mum, as well as earning a living, and you worry that this isn't possible. How, you ask yourself, will it affect my child? Will I be happy? Leaving your child at any time – baby, toddler, school-age – can be difficult. But that doesn't mean it's wrong or that your children will suffer. Take a look around you – chances are you already have plenty of inspiring friends and colleagues who not only work but have happy and thriving children, too.

How do they do it? There's no quick or easy answer – there are so many different and creative ways you can manage your home and working life. Negotiating family-friendly working hours could be part of the solution, for example. Time and how well you manage it will almost definitely be a factor. Vital, too, is an understanding of your child's needs – and how they change.

Experience also counts for a huge amount. The first few weeks or months are bound to be difficult. But once you are confident that your child is being well cared for, and your home and work life settle down, you'll feel happy with your decision. And if not? Remember that at any time you can reconsider your situation, and find ways to make changes.

We've tried in this book to give you the information, advice, strategies and shared experiences you need to discover how best to make your working life work for you and your family. And while it goes without saying that these years will probably be the most hectic in your life – hopefully they will also be the happiest.

When you are writing about children, it's really annoying to keep using 'he or she' and 'him or her' – and annoying to read too. For this reason we have switched between the two from chapter to chapter. We hope we are way beyond believing that boys can't cook and girls don't know the offside rule, so whether you have sons or daughters or both, we are sure you can substitute 'he' or 'she' as necessary.

CHAPTER 1

What is a Great Working Mum?

In a perfect world, a great working mum is someone who effortlessly creates a perfect balance between her home life and her working life, moving seamlessly between both existences, always remembering to pack her child's lunch box, always managing to get to work on time, and always having a smile on her face.

Of course, in reality, for most of us who work, each day is more work/life wobble than work/life balance as we struggle to juggle our careers with all those other jobs – cook, nurse, teacher, counsellor, mediator, taxi driver, careers adviser – that being a mum entails.

But if, occasionally, you put salami in your child's sandwiches because you've forgotten it's ham he loves, leave your briefcase at home, and look more manic mummy than yummy mummy, does it really matter?

Of course not. No mum – working or otherwise – can be perfect. Even trying would make you miserable, as it would mean never making a mistake. And with such a broad portfolio of responsibilities, getting it wrong sometimes, and not always having the answers, is inevitable.

But while no working mum can be perfect, every working mum can be great. How? By finding ways to deal with the stress, workload and time deficit that often comes with being a working mum, leaving you emotionally – and physically – free to enjoy your job, and be a relaxed, warm and loving mum. Here, in no particular order, are some tried and tested ways to achieve this, and more …

Feel confident about your choices

Guilt seems to be the norm for working mums. But is it really necessary? If you believe that you are working for legitimate reasons, then are you doing anything wrong? Feelings of guilt can only have a negative impact, not only on your own sense of self-worth, but also – if feeling guilty makes you unhappy or bad-tempered – on your children. If your reasons for working make sense, try hard to offload feelings of guilt by reminding yourself that you made your choices for good reasons.

Make good childcare a priority

Finding and keeping good childcare takes time, energy and lots of emotional input. Often it involves compromises, too. Perhaps you need to travel further than you'd ideally wish to take your child to a wonderful childminder, or spend more money than you'd hoped on a brilliant nursery. But once you've found a loving, safe and stimulating environment for your child, the transition between being at home and returning to work will be easier for you and your child.

Get organised

Being organised gives you the chance to maximise the time you can spend enjoying life with your family. You are probably used to organising your working day – meeting deadlines, making appointments, prioritising your work. And while no one wants to run their home life like a military manoeuvre, putting some simple systems in place – setting up an internet account for your supermarket shopping, keeping a notebook handy to jot down things you need to remember – can increase your efficiency at home and help you gain the time your child needs with you.

Keep work and home separate

With e-mails and mobiles it's easier than ever to stay in contact with the office, whatever the time, wherever you are. As a result, switching off from work – both literally and mentally – can be hard. But making a clear division between your work life and home life is vital. When you are at home, remember that your working day is over, and you now need to focus 100 per cent on your family. This will reassure your child that he – and not your boss – is the most important person in your life.

Share parenting

Taking on equal responsibility for looking after your child and household tasks is good for you and your partner, and good for your child, too. You both benefit from being able to balance your work and family life better, and your child benefits from getting the undivided attention of you both. Working as a team will also help you develop a strong relationship and when you and your partner are feeling close and supportive, the stresses and strains of life with growing children are easier to handle.

Review your work/life balance regularly

Taking a fresh look every now and again at how well you are managing your work and family life is the best way to avoid small niggles or difficulties blowing up into a crisis. Are those extra hours demanded at work putting too much pressure on your partner? Is now a good time to look for a new job closer to home? Unfortunately taking time to reassess does just that – it takes time! But regular reviews can help you make the minor – and sometimes major – adjustments needed to keep your work/life balance stable.

Look after yourself

Once you are back at work it's easy to find that your every waking moment is spent either at work or caring for your child, and chances are that in the struggle to find time for everything your own needs will be the first to be sacrificed. Looking after yourself, however, is vital. Making time to eat properly, getting a good night's sleep and at least occasionally doing something you *enjoy* rather than something you have to do is hugely important. It may sound clichéd but it is true – the healthier and happier you are, the easier you will find it to cope with life's everyday demands.

> *'I always knew I'd want to go back to work after having my son. I've worked hard to get where I am and I love my job. Most of my salary goes to my nanny – but Seb loves her, so it's worth it.'*
>
> Claire, TV producer and mum to Seb, 16 months

Learning as you go

Becoming a great working mum takes times and experience and there are bound to be times when circumstances (extra demands at work, a string of broken nights) undermine your efforts. When this happens, good support strategies can do wonders for your ability to cope.

- **Talk to people who understand:** sharing your difficulties with those who know what you are going through and whom you trust (your partner, family and friends) can help you to see them in a new and often less negative light.

- **Make friends with working parents:** particularly those who have children the same age. Knowing you are not the only one facing a particular problem or challenge can make the world of difference, and they may have ideas that will help you, too.

- **Contact a helpline:** if you feel you need extra support or encouragement. There's a wide range of support groups offering free help and advice (see Sources of Further Information, page 165).

SUMMARY OF CHAPTER 1

Becoming a great working mum takes time and experience, and although you can't have a practice run you can be prepared. Start with these guiding principles:

- Be confident about your choices.
- Make good childcare a priority.
- Get organised.
- Keep work and home life separate.
- Share parenting with your partner.
- Review your work/life balance regularly.
- Look after yourself.

CHAPTER 2

Pregnancy: You and Your Bump at Work

As you may already have discovered, pregnancy and work aren't always a good mix. It's no fun strap-hanging on a crowded bus when you are racked with morning sickness, and there will be days when all you can think about is curling up under your desk for a nap. Coping with pregnancy symptoms like these is particularly difficult if you've decided to keep your pregnancy private until you've had your first scan.

Realistically, you will have to do a certain amount of soldiering on during those early weeks. But there are also a few useful strategies you can use to help you survive the 'nine to five' while you're expecting. Eating well and getting plenty of rest are a good start. If things get really tough, you'll find it helpful to take a close colleague, possibly someone who's a mum, into your confidence. Keeping such a big secret can be a lonely experience and it's a great help knowing there's someone there who you can turn to in a crisis.

Coping with the early weeks

It may be one of the most exciting things that's ever happened to you, but if you're like most newly expectant mums, you probably won't want to tell a soul about your pregnancy just yet. That's fine if your pregnancy is plain sailing, but if you are overwhelmed by morning sickness and tiredness, keeping your pregnancy from your workmates can be a real trial.

One way to help keep morning sickness at bay is to have a breakfast that's rich in wholegrain carbohydrates before you go to work. The fact that so many pregnant women feel sick first thing in the morning is thought to be linked to the drop in blood-sugar levels we all experience overnight. Eating wholegrain cereal or toast will give you a sustained release of energy and help to keep your blood-sugar level stable throughout the morning. If you really can't face breakfast first thing in the morning, keep some bread or cereal at work to have when you get in.

Other tried and tested ways to beat morning sickness include ginger (in any form), vitamin B6 (do make sure the supplement you choose is suitable for pregnancy and contains no more than 10mg) and anti-histamine tablets, which your GP can prescribe. Some women swear by acupressure bands designed to relieve nausea, although these will need to be hidden under long sleeves if you don't want to arouse suspicion!

Unfortunately, there's very little you can do to relieve tiredness in the early weeks of pregnancy. It may seem obvious, but the simplest way to manage is to make sure you get to bed early at night and to rest and nap whenever you can during the day. Also try to cut back on any overtime or evening work, and keep your blood-sugar level up during the day with healthy snacks, such as bananas, yoghurts and almonds (this will help to keep nausea at bay, too).

Other work survival tactics that may be useful during early pregnancy include the following:

- Keep your desk drawer well stocked with healthy snacks, such as fruit, nuts, dried fruit, cereal bars and rice cakes (avoid peanuts if you have a family history of allergies).

- Rest whenever you can, even if it's just ten minutes with your feet up.

- Have lunch with friends and work colleagues rather than meeting up after work – this will help to hide the fact that you are not drinking alcohol, too!

- Go for a walk during your lunch hour to get some fresh air.

- Do some simple stretches and take some deep breaths at your desk whenever you start to nod off.

If pregnancy niggles are really making work impossible – if you are constantly having to run to the loo to be sick, for example – do confide in someone. If you don't want your line manager to know just yet, this could be a close work colleague (someone who is also a mother, perhaps) or someone in human resources. If you want to keep any conversations you have about your pregnancy confidential, do make this clear from the start.

If all else fails, consider telling your employer about your pregnancy (see page 25) as, once you've done this, your employer is legally obliged to offer you regular rest periods during the day.

'There's no question – those first few weeks at work were really tough. I coped by resting lots at weekends and having naps when I got in from work while Mark cooked the supper. At work I'd just get my head down and count the minutes until home time.'

Marianne, advertising account manager
and 28 weeks pregnant

Staying safe and comfortable

Once you've told your employer about your pregnancy, they are legally obliged to give you a health and safety assessment to make sure you and your baby are safe at work. You should be fully involved in this assessment and, among other things, your employer must check that:

- your workstation is safe and comfortable

- there are adequate facilities for you to rest

- your hours are reasonable

- you do not have to lift heavy loads

- you are not exposed to potentially harmful chemicals

- you are not unduly stressed

- you are not at risk of violence.

Your employer is also expected to take the particular conditions of your pregnancy into account. If you are suffering from morning sickness, for example, it's unreasonable to expect you to do early-morning shifts. Or, if you have backache, you shouldn't have to stand for long periods. You may need to ask your doctor for a letter to confirm your symptoms.

Once any risks have been identified, they must be removed where possible. If the risks can't be removed, your employer must adjust your working conditions or hours so that you are no longer exposed to any risk. If this isn't possible, you should be offered suitable alternative work with the same terms and conditions or, failing that, be suspended on full pay for as long as necessary.

You may also like to try these simple tips to keep you and your baby safe and comfortable:

- **Take lots of breaks:** sit down if you have to stand a lot, or get up and walk around if you are sitting for most of the day.

- **Move your legs:** when sitting, stretch your legs, rotate your ankles and wriggle your toes now and again to keep your blood moving.

- **Try to eat proper meals:** rather than snacking. Also make sure you drink plenty of non-caffeinated drinks such as water, fruit juice, milk and herbal tea.

- **Dress sensibly:** stick to sensible flatties for work and dress in layers as you'll tend to feel warmer as your pregnancy progresses.

- **Try to avoid stressful situations:** stress isn't good for unborn babies or their mums.

- **Keep a note of your midwife's phone number:** keep this with you at work and call her if you are worried about anything.

Pregnancy complications

There are a number of pregnancy complications that may require you to take time off work to safeguard your own and your baby's health: if, for example, you've previously had more than one premature baby, you have diabetes or high blood pressure, have a history of miscarriage or are expecting twins. If this is the case, your GP may put you on sick leave.

Miscarriage

The most common pregnancy complication is miscarriage (when a pregnancy ends before 24 weeks). Around one in five pregnancies end in miscarriage, with most occurring during the first 12 weeks.

Miscarrying very early in pregnancy often requires no treatment, although sometimes a minor operation may be necessary to empty the uterus. You may, however, still need time to recover – both physically and emotionally. Your GP can sign you off sick for as long as necessary; sick leave related to a miscarriage is protected in the same way as sick leave for any other pregnancy-related illness.

Miscarriage can be a trauma, even when it occurs early in the pregnancy. So although you may not yet have told your employer that you were pregnant, it may be easier if colleagues at work know what's happened and understand why you may be less cheerful or engaged than usual.

Stillbirth and neonatal death

Stillbirth (when a baby is born dead after the 24th week of pregnancy) and neonatal death (when a baby is born alive at any stage of the pregnancy but dies under the age of 28 days) are both very rare. In the UK only about one baby in every 200 is stillborn and about one in 300 dies in the first four weeks of life. The main causes of stillbirth are infection, placental problems, problems with the mother's health, congenital malformations and complications surrounding the umbilical cord. The main causes of neonatal death are prematurity and low birth weight.

Whatever the reason, however, you will need a great deal of time and support to deal with a stillbirth.

- Get a friend or family member to tell everyone who needs to know – including your boss – what has happened. It's too much to expect you or your partner to have to go through the details again and again.

- Even though your baby was stillborn, you still have all the maternity rights – maternity leave and pay – you would have had if your baby had been born alive. If the birth happens before you intended to start maternity leave, or before the 25th week of pregnancy (in the case where your baby is born alive but then dies), you will need to inform your employer as soon as you can.

- If your partner is eligible for paternity leave, he will still be entitled to take this after a stillbirth.

- Although you can stay off work for your full maternity leave, you don't have to – going back to work and having something to focus on may give you relief from your grief.

- Your first day back at work will be nerve-racking – you are leaving the security of your home, and are fearful of how people will react to you, and you to them. It may be a good idea to make a short visit – a couple of mornings, for example, to ease yourself into your old routine.

- If people avoid you, try not to take it personally. For those who have never experienced loss, knowing what to say or do can be difficult. There is often the worry that mentioning it will bring back the sorrow, although most parents who have experienced stillbirth agree that they would rather their loss were acknowledged than ignored.

- Don't expect too much of yourself – it's inevitable that you'll tire quickly, be forgetful, lose concentration and for a while work on automatic pilot.

- For support from other parents who have also experienced stillbirth or neonatal death, contact SANDS, the Stillbirth and Neonatal Death Society (see Sources of Further Information, page 165).

'When Madeleine died, I invited some of my close work colleagues to the funeral. I think being there helped them understand what I was going through and made it easier for me when I went back to work.'

Milly, primary school teacher and mum to Madeleine, and Tom, three

Late pregnancy

For many expectant mums, the last few weeks of work can seem to last forever. Your bump will probably feel huge and you may be suffering with common late-pregnancy problems like backache, breathlessness and heartburn. Work is probably hectic, too, as you prepare to hand over, and you may be starting to wonder why on earth you didn't start your maternity leave sooner.

If pregnancy-related problems or just the sheer effort of commuting and working become too much for you, you may want to consider taking some annual leave to start your maternity leave earlier. You could also ask your GP to sign you off sick, but do bear in mind that, if you are off sick with a pregnancy-related condition in the four weeks leading up to your due date, your employer can insist that you start your maternity leave immediately.

If pregnancy-related ailments are making life difficult, there are some steps you can take to improve matters.

Backache

If you sit down a lot during the day, make sure your chair is set at the right height for your desk and that it supports your lower back properly. You should already have had a full health and safety assessment, but don't be afraid to ask for your workstation to be assessed again. If your feet don't rest comfortably on the ground once your chair is adjusted, you'll need a footrest. If you stand for long periods at work, make sure you sit down regularly. Finally, it hardly needs saying, but do avoid lifting heavy objects.

Heartburn and indigestion

A poor diet, eating too fast, eating too much and eating spicy, oily or acidic foods can all aggravate these common late-pregnancy problems. The trick is to eat small, healthy meals regularly, so plan ahead and take a couple of tasty meals into work with you each morning. Homemade sandwiches, salads, pasta and soups are ideal.

Needing to pee frequently

Frequent trips to the loo can become a fact of life as your growing baby starts to press on your bladder. Do keep your fluid intake up, as limiting your fluids to save yourself a trip to the toilet will only make you more prone to urine infections and could leave you dehydrated.

Varicose veins

Hormonal changes make you more prone to varicose veins when you are pregnant, and standing for long periods only exacerbates the problem. If you suffer in this way, try wearing support socks and sitting with your feet raised above hip level whenever you can.

Leaking breasts

It's a little-known fact that your breasts can start to leak in late pregnancy as they gear up for breastfeeding. The solution is simple: buy yourself some breastpads (you can get washable or disposable) and keep them in your desk drawer along with a clean bra and top to change into if necessary.

'I felt incredibly heavy and breathless and couldn't wait for my last day to come. But when it arrived I felt quite sad saying goodbye to everyone. I've told them all that I will bring the baby to see them, and they've promised to keep me up to date with all the gossip.'

Moira, visual merchandising specialist
and 37 weeks pregnant

As your last day of work approaches, take the time to tie up any loose ends. If you have regular supervisions with your manager, make sure you have one before you leave so that your performance record is up to date when you come back, and try to get round all your main contacts to let them know that you will be away for a while. If you are happy to do so, let them know how you can be contacted while you are away. Make sure you have a proper handover with your replacement, too – you don't want endless phone calls while you are trying to breathe through contractions or breastfeed. Then it's time to clear out your drawers, raise a glass of sparkling water with your colleagues and wave goodbye to work and hello to motherhood.

SUMMARY OF CHAPTER 2

- Keep healthy snacks in your drawer and make sure you get plenty of rest when you can.
- Keep fatigue at bay with stretches at your desk or a brisk walk at lunchtime.
- If you are finding work a struggle, confide in a close colleague who can offer you support.
- Make sure you are given a proper health and safety assessment so that you can stay safe and comfortable at work.
- Miscarriage, even in the early stages of pregnancy, can be traumatic. If you need it, take sick leave to give yourself time to recover.
- Stillbirth and neonatal death are very rare but devastating when they do happen. You will be deeply shocked and will need lots of emotional support plus plenty of time to grieve.
- Take good care of yourself as your pregnancy advances and your last day at work approaches, and allow yourself plenty of time to do a proper handover.

Chapter 3

Your Maternity Rights: Get What You Need

Whatever your circumstances, it's vital that you swot up on your maternity rights. At times the information is complicated and, yes, downright dull, but not all employers are up to speed with maternity entitlements so you'll need to take the initiative. You'll find plenty of information on the internet, making it easier for you to do some discreet research before you speak to your employer.

Telling the boss that you are pregnant is always a worrying prospect. Don't leave it too long, though, as most of the special privileges you enjoy as a pregnant woman, including time off for antenatal appointments, don't kick in until you've done so. You may be pleasantly surprised at how well your news is received in any case.

Telling your employer

In order to qualify for maternity leave, you need to tell your employer you are pregnant by the fifteenth week before your baby is due. This is known as your 'qualifying week'. For maternity-leave purposes, weeks start on a Sunday so, to pinpoint your qualifying week, just start on the Sunday before your due date (or actually on your due date if it's a Sunday), then count back 15 weeks.

Although your employer needs to know about your pregnancy by the qualifying week, there are good reasons for telling him or her earlier. One is that your employer can make life easier for you if morning sickness, tiredness and other pregnancy-related problems are making work impossible. You may be able to negotiate a later start time to avoid the rush hour, for example, or perhaps the chance to work from home occasionally. You are also protected against any unfair treatment related to your pregnancy (including dismissal) once you've told your employer, and can take paid leave for antenatal appointments.

If you work for a small employer, it's particularly important to give plenty of warning that you are planning to take maternity leave. A recent survey by the Equal Opportunities Commission found that the average small employer only has one pregnant employee about every ten years. Because of this, lots of small employers are unclear about maternity rights. They're also more likely to struggle with the cost of covering your maternity leave. Giving plenty of notice helps to ensure that your rights as an expectant mum aren't overlooked, as well as helping your employer to plan ahead.

> *'I thought my manager would go mad when I told her I was pregnant, but she was very nice about it. She's going to organise a proper health and safety assessment for me and she said I could take as much time off for antenatal appointments as I need.'*
>
> Lauren, finance executive and ten weeks pregnant

Your maternity leave and pay

In order to qualify for maternity leave and pay, there are four things you need to do:

- Tell your employer you are pregnant.

- Say when you want your maternity leave and pay to start.

- Give notice in writing if your employer asks you to (all that's needed is a simple letter stating that you are pregnant, the date your baby's due and when you'd like to start your maternity leave).

- Give your employer the MATB1 certificate confirming when your baby is due – your midwife will give you this some time after week 20.

Once you've done these things, your employer then has to write to you within 28 days to confirm when you'll be due back at work. The dates you give your employer aren't set in stone: you can change your mind about when you want to start your maternity leave as long as you give your employer at least 28 days' warning.

You can start your maternity leave any time from 11 weeks before your baby is due. Most expectant mums work for as long as possible so that they can have more time with their baby. In theory you can work right up to your due date, but given that lots of babies are born before their due dates, this probably isn't a good idea! Bear in mind, too, that you may be tired and uncomfortable during those last few weeks, making work and commuting increasingly difficult.

What you are entitled to

If you are an employee, you are entitled to 52 weeks' maternity leave regardless of how long you've worked for your employer or how many hours you work. During the first 26 weeks, you'll have exactly the same rights as if you were working. During the last 26 weeks only some of your rights will continue, such as your right to redundancy pay if you are made redundant. Do check your contract, though, because some employers let you keep full contractual rights all through your maternity leave.

Most pregnant employees are entitled to Statutory Maternity Pay (SMP), which is paid for 39 weeks. You qualify for SMP if you were already working for your employer before you got pregnant and if you earn enough to pay National Insurance. You'll usually get 90 per cent of your average earnings for the first six weeks and then the current flat rate for the remaining 33 weeks (bear in mind that you'll have to pay tax and National Insurance on this).

If you don't qualify for SMP, or if you are self-employed, you may be entitled to Maternity Allowance (MA). Like SMP, this is paid for 39 weeks. To qualify for MA, you need to have worked for at least 26 out of the 66 weeks leading up to the week your baby is due. You also need to have paid National Insurance in any 13 weeks during the same period.

What your partner's entitled to

Most expectant dads who are employees are entitled to one or two weeks of paternity leave. To qualify, your partner needs to have been working for his employer before you got pregnant. He also has to tell his employer in writing that he's intending to take paternity leave before the qualifying week (see Telling your employer, page 25). Paternity leave has to be taken within 56 days of your baby's birth and, if your partner takes two weeks, these have to be taken consecutively.

Most men who qualify for paternity leave are also entitled to Statutory Paternity Pay. This will either be the current flat rate or 90 per cent of average weekly earnings if this is lower. Your partner needs to tell his employer when he wants his paternity pay at least 28 days in advance, but in practice it's probably easiest to give written notice of both paternity leave *and* pay by the qualifying week.

> *'Paternity pay isn't great, but we decided James would go ahead and take some paternity leave anyway. I'm so glad we did. Those first few weeks with Ruby were amazing, but they were exhausting as well and I'd have been lost without him.'*
>
> Becca, website designer and mum to Ruby, five months

If you are adopting

If you are an employee and are adopting a child through an agency, you may be entitled to adoption pay and leave. This is available to people who are adopting a child on their own or for one member of a couple who are adopting. Unfortunately, you don't get pay or leave for other kinds of adoption, such as the adoption of a stepchild, or if you are self-employed.

If you are adopting from within the UK, you need to have worked for your employer for at least 26 weeks when you are matched with your child to qualify for adoption leave. You'll also have to give your employer proof (usually a certificate from the adoption agency) to show you have the right to paid leave. If you are adopting from abroad, you need to tell your employer that you are planning to take adoption leave within 28 days of getting your official notification. This is usually a certificate from the Department of Health confirming that you have been approved as a suitable adoptive parent.

Like maternity leave, adoption leave is 52 weeks long. Statutory Adoption Pay (SAP) lasts 39 weeks, and is paid either at the current flat rate or as 90 per cent of your earnings, whichever is lower.

Your rights during pregnancy

Pregnant women are generally well protected at work in the UK. If you become ill with a pregnancy-related condition, for example, your employer must pay you in the same way as for any other kind of sickness. You are also excluded from your employer's normal sickness-related disciplinary rules.

You are entitled to time off for antenatal appointments while you are pregnant, and that includes time spent travelling and waiting to be seen. An antenatal appointment is considered to be any appointment you make on the advice of your doctor, midwife or health visitor, including relaxation or parentcraft classes.

It is also illegal for you to be treated unfairly at work because of your pregnancy or because you want to take maternity leave. If you are dismissed while you are pregnant, you have to be given written reasons. You can still be made redundant while you are pregnant, but, again, the reasons for redundancy can't be connected in any way with your pregnancy or a pregnancy-related illness.

Discrimination at work

Sadly, for many women, being pregnant at work is an unhappy experience because their bosses do not understand how to manage them. A recent Equal Opportunities Commission investigation found that almost half of pregnant working women experience some disadvantage in the workplace as a result of pregnancy or maternity leave. This can include indirect discrimination – for example, being refused a more appropriate shift schedule – as well as direct discrimination, such as being sacked or threatened with dismissal by employers for becoming pregnant, being denied the chance to go for a promotion while pregnant and being made redundant while on maternity leave.

Discrimination on the grounds of pregnancy is, however, illegal. As we've already mentioned, the law says you must not be treated less favourably because you are pregnant, or because you are going to take maternity leave.

So what can you do to protect yourself? And what can you do if the worst happens?

- Once you know you are pregnant, check that you know exactly what you have to do under law to benefit from the protection that's there for you (like time off for antenatal appointments, maternity leave, etc). For further information, check out the government leaflet *Pregnancy and Work: What you need to know as an employee*, which you can find under Related Documents at www.berr.gov.uk/employment/workandfamilies.

- Make sure your employer is properly informed about the rights of pregnant women – the above leaflet has a section especially intended for pregnant women to give to their employers.

- Talk to your employer about your plans from an early stage.

- Don't automatically assume your employer is acting unreasonably – if there is a problem, it might be a simple mistake or misunderstanding.

- Try to resolve difficulties informally – talk first with your line manager, personnel department, colleagues or trade union.

Keep detailed notes in case later on you need to establish exactly what was discussed.

- If the problem can't be resolved, you may have to make a formal complaint under the grievance procedure. You can get free advice about this from Working Families. Call their helpline on 0800 013 0313 or visit www.working families.org.uk. Alternatively, contact ACAS and/or the Citizens Advice Bureau (see Sources of Further Information, page 165).

- If the situation still can't be resolved, you may decide to take your case to an employment tribunal.

'Since I've become pregnant I need to go to the loo so often. I have a difficult relationship with my line manager, and she'd often refuse my request to leave my workstation. I had to talk to the personnel department about the situation and, happily, they were able to help sort it out.'

Fran, booking agent and seven months pregnant

SUMMARY OF CHAPTER 3

- Expectant mums' rights are better than they've ever been, so make sure you get clued up on what you are entitled to.

- To qualify for maternity leave, you'll need to tell your employer that you are expecting 15 weeks before the week in which your baby is due.

- Do tell you employer about your pregnancy earlier rather than later, so that they can plan ahead and you can take full advantage of what you are entitled to.

- Dads have rights, too, these days so it's well worth checking out what paternity pay and leave your partner may be entitled to.

- If you are an employee and you are adopting a child through an agency, you may be entitled to adoption leave and pay.

CHAPTER 4

Maternity Leave: Making the Most of It

Most mothers look back on their maternity leave as one of the most enjoyable periods of their lives. Released from the pressures of work, you'll have plenty of time to rest, relax and get to know your new baby once she arrives. Hopefully, your partner will be entitled to some paternity leave, too, so that you can enjoy spending time with your baby together.

Once your partner goes back to work, though, you may feel a little lonely. It can be hard to get used to a quiet life that revolves around your baby when you are accustomed to the hectic pace of working life. This is the time to get in touch with friends who also have babies or to strike up new friendships with other new mums in your area. If you are not sure where to start, your midwife or health visitor should be able to tell you about mother-and-baby groups local to you.

While rest and relaxation are vital, there are a few important bits of paperwork you'll need to think about while you are on maternity leave. These include the claim forms for your baby's Child Trust Fund and Child Benefit, plus any tax credits you may be entitled to. It's also a good idea to check in with work now and again. They'll be dying to hear all your baby news, and it will mean you don't feel quite as out of the loop when you return.

As a working mum you'll almost certainly receive some kind of maternity pay while you are on maternity leave, but this will probably be a fraction of what you are normally paid. While life with a small baby tends to be quite inexpensive, you may need to tighten your belt for a while. Making sure you are getting the best possible deals on your mortgage, insurance and other bills is a good place to start.

But, above all, cherish this precious time with your baby. At times, the days may seem long, but before you know it your maternity leave will be over and it'll be time to face the joys and challenges of being a working mum.

Making good use of your maternity leave

For most women, maternity leave comes as a welcome release from early rising, commuting and sandwich lunches. Without the pressures of work and with plenty of time to rest, the weeks before your baby is born should be some of the happiest of your life, so make the most of them.

- **Stock up the freezer:** take this opportunity to cook some hearty homemade meals and stack them up in the freezer to enjoy after your baby is born. As a new mother, you need to be well nourished and you certainly won't have time to spend hours in the kitchen preparing wholesome meals.

- **Enjoy nesting:** lots of women say they feel an urge to 'nest' in the last few weeks of pregnancy, but it's important not to overdo it. Washing and sorting tiny little clothes, packing your hospital bag and spring-cleaning your bedroom is fine. Making a dash round the shopping centre eight days past your due date is not.

- **Cherish this time with your partner:** soon your cosy twosome will be a sleepless threesome, and nights out and lazy lie-ins will just be a distant memory. Whether it's the theatre, cinema, gigs or meals out that you enjoy, take this opportunity to relax and enjoy each other's company.

- **Spend time with friends:** nights out and long, boozy dinners won't be an option for a while so now's a good time to look up any friends you haven't seen for a while.

- **Book yourself into a beauty salon:** getting a haircut now means you won't have to worry about making another hair appointment for a while. And treat yourself to a massage or facial while you're at it – again, you won't have much opportunity to pamper yourself over the next few months.

- **Put a message on your answerphone:** as your due date approaches, you'll find you are inundated by phonecalls from anxious friends and relatives wanting to know the latest. Leaving a message along the lines of, 'No, baby Simpson hasn't arrived yet, but we'll let you know just as soon as she does' should help to reassure people.

- **Rest, rest, rest:** once you are breastfeeding five times a night you'll regret every second you didn't spend resting or asleep before your baby arrived. Plenty of rest will also help you to build up stamina for your baby's birth.

'I loved being on maternity leave. I'll never forget how happy and excited I felt looking at a row of little sleepsuits drying on the washing line. I felt incredibly close to Mick, too. It was just a lovely time.'

Michelle, travel manager and mum to Liam, 14 months

Bonding with your baby

For some new mums, bonding begins as soon as they meet their baby for the first time. For others, feelings of love can take many months to emerge. Perhaps you had a difficult birth or your baby needed special care. Perhaps she isn't the sex you longed for or she doesn't look as you'd imagined.

Try not to worry, as during your maternity leave you'll have plenty of time to get to know your baby and adjust to motherhood. It's important to talk about your feelings to your partner, your midwife or a close friend, too. Many women have the same feelings as you – they don't mean you are a bad mother or abnormal – and sharing them with others can help.

Occasionally difficulties in bonding may signal postnatal depression. This may be hard to recognise in yourself so it's important to discuss any negative feelings with your partner, midwife or GP or someone else you feel close to. Getting the right kind of help as soon as possible is vital to your recovery.

Taking time to get to know your baby is one of the best ways to help you develop a close and loving relationship.

- **Enjoy your baby:** there's no rush. These are precious times so relish the day-to-day physical tasks such as dressing, feeding, bathing and changing. Marvelling at her tiny body, stroking her gently, holding her close – all this will help to stimulate your protective feelings, as well as having a wonderfully relaxing effect on her.

- **Touch your baby:** skin-to-skin contact is one of the most powerful ways you can get to know her and helps to form a strong emotional bond. Set aside peaceful times (perhaps after feeding) when you can hold your baby against your skin and enjoy a sense of closeness.

- **Talk to your baby:** even though she's just been born, your baby will respond to the sound of your voice, turning her head, wiggling and kicking.

- **Look at your baby:** when you hold her in your arms (20–25cm/8–10in away) she can focus on your face and make eye contact.

Meeting other mums

You'll probably find that the first few weeks after your baby's birth fly by in a wonderful haze of hormones, tiredness, feeding and nappy changing. But once the congratulations cards stop dropping onto the doormat and your partner returns to work, it's natural to find yourself feeling a little bored and possibly lonely at times. Adapting to the quiet baby-centred life of a new mum can be a challenge when you are used to the hustle and bustle – not to mention adult conversation – of a busy workplace. You may also have concerns about your own and your baby's well-being that you'd like to share with others.

Now's the time to think about hooking up with other new mums in your area. Wherever you live, there are bound to be other mothers out there who are just as keen to make new friends. Being a mum breaks down barriers between people, and lots of strong, enduring friendships have been struck up over conversations about colic, nappy rash and solids. You may well find that the friendships you make now form the basis of an invaluable support network as your baby grows into childhood.

Your midwife or health visitor should be able to tell you what groups and activities are available for new mums in your area. Or you could try the notice board in your GP's surgery when you take your baby for her check-ups. Your local Sure Start or Children's Centre is another good place to make enquiries, and lots of women meet other new mums through their local branch of the National Childbirth Trust (NCT).

Swimming, yoga, mother-and-baby film clubs, baby signing, baby massage and buggy strolls are just some of the other activities available for mums and babies. There are also specialist groups available if you prefer, including groups for mums who are older or younger, mums who have twins, mums who are breastfeeding or who have postnatal depression. The internet is another great source of support and advice and lots of new mums now bond in internet chat rooms and on bulletin boards. Some websites also have regional boards so that mums can meet up locally if they wish.

'We moved house while I was pregnant with Kiera, so I didn't know anyone in my area. But I made some really good friends through a baby swimming class at my local pool. We'd all go for a coffee afterwards and compare notes and chat. Now I'm back at work, but we still meet up for swims at the weekend.'

Fiona, personal trainer and mum to Kiera, 13 months

Managing your money

You'll be amazed how far your money stretches once you are on maternity leave and, if you think about it, it makes sense. You are no longer paying for your commute to work or for all those sandwich-shop lunches. No more birthday collections in the office or expensive coffees or lunches out. And unless your role model is Victoria Beckham, you won't be spending too much on haircuts, make-up and clothes for a while, either.

Even so, the fact is that you'll have to survive on significantly less money while you are on maternity leave. Plus, once you go back to work, you may well be paying for childcare, which doesn't come cheap. Now is a good time to take a long, hard look at your finances to see where you can make some savings and get yourself into better financial habits.

- **Give yourself a financial overhaul:** take a good look at all your outgoings – mortgage, bills, insurance and so on – and see where you may be able to make some savings. Comparison websites such as www.uswitch.com can be helpful or, alternatively, make an appointment with an independent financial adviser for a financial MOT.

- **Work out a budget:** work out how much maternity pay you will be getting and add that figure to any savings you made while you were pregnant. Then subtract all your important outgoings over the coming months. Set yourself a weekly budget based on what's left and stick to it.

- **Prioritise your treats:** decide which treats you are going to keep in your life and which ones can go – you may decide to ditch the taxis and takeaways, for example, but keep the magazines and rented DVDs.

- **Get what you are entitled to:** make sure you get all the benefits and payments you are eligible for as a new parent (see What to claim for your baby, page 39).

- **Buy second hand:** baby gear is expensive, but you can save a fortune by buying only the essentials new and buying bigger items second hand (the one exception to this is cot mattresses, which should always be bought new).

- **Think about taking some payment holidays:** some mortgage and pension providers allow you to lower your payments or stop them altogether for a limited period – check with your providers and consider changing products if your current ones don't allow this.

- **Start saving:** saving your Child Benefit up for when your baby needs something is a good place to start.

- **Get out of the credit habit:** try putting your credit cards away while you are on maternity leave or, even better, cut them up. While you are at home with a baby, you won't have much opportunity for impulse buys in any case.

'I've got into the habit of borrowing DVDs, books and CDs from the local library. It gets us out of the house and it's amazing how much money I've saved.'

Quita, special needs co-ordinator and mum to Rosa, six months

What to claim for your baby

You are entitled to a range of benefits, tax credits and other payments once your baby's born and it's important that you don't miss out on them. They include Child Benefit, Child Tax Credit, Working Tax Credit and the Child Trust Fund.

- **Child Benefit:** just about everyone with children under the age of 16 is entitled to Child Benefit and you can start claiming as soon as your baby is born. You should get a claim form in the Bounty pack given to every new mother. Alternatively, call the Child Benefit Office on 0845 302 1444.

- **Tax credits:** Child Tax Credit is an allowance for people who have children. Working Tax Credit is for parents who work and it includes a childcare element for parents with children in childcare. Both tax credits are based on your income and you can claim them on the same form. You can get this either from your local JobCentre Plus or by phoning the Tax Credits helpline on 0845 300 3900.

- **Child Trust Fund:** under the Child Trust Fund scheme all new parents claiming Child Benefit receive a voucher worth £250 (£500 if you are on a low income). This can then be invested for your child until she reaches the age of 18. The voucher will be sent to you automatically, along with advice on how to invest it, when you claim Child Benefit. Your child will get a further payment at the age of seven.

Staying in touch with work

No matter how wrapped up you are in your baby, it's a good idea to check in with your manager and work colleagues now and again. This will help you to keep up with all the latest developments and let people know that you are still 'in the loop'. It will also mean that when you do return to work your first day back won't feel quite as strange.

Most new mums enjoy taking their baby to meet work colleagues, and this will also give you a chance to find out about any job vacancies or training opportunities that have come up while you've been away. Once your baby's a little older, why not leave her with a trusted friend or relative for a couple of hours while you enjoy a lunch out with colleagues on your own. It will be a useful practice separation for you both as well as giving you a little reminder of the dynamic working girl you once were.

'I really enjoyed taking Milo out for lunch with the girls from work. They all had a hold while I caught up with the gossip. We're going to meet up again in about a month's time and this time I'm planning to leave Milo with my mum. Perhaps she'll even get him to take a bottle of expressed milk!'

Lynda, senior personnel manager and mum to Milo, five months

If you like, you can work for your employer for up to ten days during your maternity leave without affecting your maternity leave or pay. These are known as 'keeping-in-touch days'. They can be taken at any time apart from the two weeks after your baby is born, and can be used for any work-related activity, including training, meetings, conferences and awaydays. It's up to you to negotiate with your manager about how much you get paid for these days, how many you take and when.

Your maternity leave is also a great time to learn new skills and brush up on old ones. Many community colleges have crèches and nurseries available, and you may even be entitled to reduced fees while you are receiving maternity pay.

Deciding when to go back

Before you started your maternity leave, your employer will have written to you to tell you the date you are expected back at work. In theory you can just turn up on the day, but it's obviously a good idea to get back in touch with your employer before then. You need only give your employer official notice if you decide to go back early, in other words, before 52 weeks. In this case, you'll need to give at least eight weeks' notice.

If you'd like to extend your maternity leave beyond 52 weeks, you have a couple of options. One is to take some annual leave – you'll keep accruing this during your maternity leave, so you should have some owing. Alternatively, you could take some unpaid parental leave (you can take a total of 13 weeks before your baby's fifth birthday). Do speak to your employer well in advance, though, if this is what you are planning as they will need to make sure your post is covered for a little longer.

Deciding when to return to work is a highly personal decision. You'll need to take into account your own and your baby's needs, plus the needs of your family as a whole. How you feel about your job is important: you may absolutely love your work and be desperate to return, or you may be dreading your first day back. Whatever you decide, do take your time over your decision and talk it through with your partner first. This is the first of many difficult and emotional choices you'll have to make as a working mum, and it's important that you feel happy with your decision.

SUMMARY OF CHAPTER 4

- First and foremost, your maternity leave is a precious time for you to rest, relax and get to know your baby.
- Make sure you and your baby have plenty of time, as well as peace and quiet, to bond.
- Your maternity leave is a great time to make new friends – ask your midwife or health visitor about mother-and-baby groups in your area, search for groups online or look on the notice board at your GP's surgery.
- You'll probably need to budget while you are on maternity leave, so take the opportunity to sort your finances out.
- Don't miss out on what you are entitled to – once your baby is born you can apply for several benefits and tax credits, including Child Benefit, Child Tax Credit, Working Tax Credit and the Child Trust Fund.
- It's a good idea to stay in touch with work via phone calls, lunches and possibly a few working days while you are on maternity leave – that way, going back to work won't be quite such a wrench.
- Deciding when to go back to work can be a difficult, emotional decision – give yourself plenty of time to think it through carefully.

Chapter 5

Childcare:
How to Find the Best

If enjoying time with your baby is your most important task while you are on maternity leave, finding suitable childcare comes a very close second. You probably feel appalled at the idea of handing your precious baby over to someone else when you return to work, but do remember that people who work in childcare usually do so because they love children and enjoy being with them. Childcarers are also increasingly well qualified and carefully regulated these days.

If you are wondering how being in childcare is likely to affect your child, experts generally agree that high-quality paid-for childcare can benefit children by encouraging them to be sociable and boosting their early learning skills. On the minus side, some research suggests that babies who spend long hours in childcare from a very early age are more likely to show aggressive and antisocial behaviour later on. Other studies show that babies whose mums work full time do better in paid childcare than informal childcare. You also need to bear in mind the other benefits that childcare will bring to your family, such as boosting your family income and allowing you to have a satisfying work life.

Where to begin your search

Ideally you need to start thinking about childcare while you are still pregnant or, at very least, soon after your baby is born. This may seem ridiculous, but it's absolutely true. In order for you to thrive as a working mum you'll need high-quality, reliable childcare in a convenient location and to cover the hours that suit you. This is surprisingly difficult to come by. Good nannies and childminders tend to get snapped up quickly and popular nurseries often have very long waiting lists. Starting early is especially important if your baby is disabled as suitable childcare places for children with special needs tend to be particularly scarce.

Many parents rely on word of mouth to find childcare places. While personal recommendations are incredibly helpful, what works for one family may not work for yours, so it's also important to have an overview of everything that's available in your area. The simplest way to do this is to contact your local Children's Information Service – you can get their contact details from the government's ChildcareLink website at www.childcare link.gov.uk or from their free helpline on 0800 234 6346.

Other useful places to look are the notice boards at local community centres, cafés, libraries and shops (do remember to chase up references if you use this route). Try looking under 'Childcare' in Yellow Pages, too. If you are considering hiring a nanny, you may want to look in magazines like *Nursery World* and *The Lady*, which publish details of both nanny agencies and individual nannies who are available for work.

> *'My friend recommended a good local nanny agency, but I felt I wanted to keep an open mind. I'm glad I did because we chose a nursery near where I work in the end and it's worked out really well.'*
>
> Caitlin, estate agent and mum to Romy, 14 months

What's available

Once you've found out what's available in your area, you'll be able to start narrowing down your options. The list below of the various pros and cons of each sort of childcare may help. Au pairs aren't included as they are usually inexperienced and unqualified and, as such, are not suitable carers for babies unless, perhaps, you work from home and so are available to handle any crises that come up (for information about au pairs, see Childcare for older children, page 54).

Childminders

Many childminders are mums who start caring for other people's children in their own homes when their own children are small. They are allowed to care for up to six children under eight, although only three can be under five. Almost all childminders are Ofsted registered and, as such, they have to undergo a Criminal Records Bureau (CRB) check, basic childcare training (including first aid) and annual inspections. Childminders tend to charge reasonable rates and are the second most popular form of childcare in the UK after care by relatives. Many families consider their childminder 'one of the family' and enjoy warm relationships with them.

Pros

- Childminders can give your baby lots of one-to-one attention as they only look after a small number of children.

- With their small, mixed-age groups of children and homely settings, childminders can offer a home-from-home experience particularly suited to young children.

- Childminders tend to be more flexible about hours and ad hoc care than nurseries – some even take children overnight and at weekends.

- Most childminders do school drop-offs and pick-ups and can look after your baby right up to secondary-school age if necessary.

- Childminders are self-employed and look after their own tax and National Insurance.

Cons

- Childminders are generally not as highly qualified as nursery staff or nannies.

- You may be left in the lurch if your childminder falls ill or goes on holiday, although many have reciprocal arrangements with other local childminders to cover these eventualities.

- Your child will have to fit in with your childminder's routine and lifestyle to some extent.

- A childminder may not provide as many early-learning opportunities as a nursery, although they are required to provide stimulating age-appropriate activities for all the children in their care.

Day nurseries

Day nurseries offer childcare for pre-school children provided by trained, professional staff working in a purpose-built environment. Nurseries must have a certain ratio of carers to children: for under-twos this is one carer to every three children. Nursery hours vary, but most cater for working parents and are open between around 8am and 6pm. Nurseries can be private, council-run or in the workplace, but all have to be registered with Ofsted.

Pros

- Nurseries offer a safe, stimulating environment with professional childcarers.

- The fact that the children are of similar ages helps to build their confidence and encourage friendships.

- Nurseries also give you the opportunity to meet and befriend other parents.

- Most nurseries are open all year round, so you don't have to worry about what to do in the event of sickness or holidays.

- Most nursery staff are trained in early years education and will be able to monitor and encourage your child's development.

● Some parents like the structured routine and clear rules that nurseries offer.

Cons

● Nursery places can be very hard to come by in some areas, especially for babies.

● A nursery may be unwilling to take children who are under the weather or have something contagious.

● Dropping-off and picking-up hours are often rigid and some nurseries issue fines for late pick-ups.

● Some parents find a nursery environment too impersonal for babies.

● Nursery fees can be high.

● Because nurseries care for larger groups of children, your baby is more likely to pick up coughs, colds and other bugs.

'We chose a nursery for Colin because we liked that fact that he had lots of other children to play with. It helps that they're open all year round as well.'

Sue, nutritionist and mum to Colin, three

Nannies

A nanny is usually a qualified, experienced childcare professional who will come to your home to care for your child or possibly live in. She (or he) will usually be there to dress and feed your child in the morning and will care for her until you return from work. In most cases, you will be the nanny's employer, which means you'll need to pay her income tax and National Insurance. It's not compulsory for nannies to be registered with Ofsted, but they can apply to join the voluntary part of Ofsted's Childcare Register. In order to be included they must meet certain basic standards set out by Ofsted. Parents who employ a nanny who is on the voluntary register are entitled to claim the childcare element of the Working Tax Credit (see Help with the cost, page 53).

Pros

- Your baby will get lots of one-to-one attention.

- Most nannies are well qualified.

- Your baby will be cared for in the comfort and security of your own home.

- Most nannies are happy to take on other bits of housework, such as washing and ironing your child's clothes, babysitting and walking the dog.

- Nannies are very convenient if your job demands flexibility in your hours.

- If your child is under the weather, you always have the option of leaving her at home with your nanny.

- You'll have lots of control over what your nanny does with your child, the daily routine and food.

Cons

- Nannies can be an expensive option, especially if you only have one child, but some families spread the cost by setting up nanny shares (see Help with the cost, page 53).

- Nannies are not always registered with Ofsted so you may not be able to get money back through the tax credit system.

- As an employer, you will have to give your nanny a contract, offer her paid leave and pay her tax and National Insurance. You will also have to keep all the relevant paperwork in order.

- Your child may only have limited contact with other children.

- If you are considering a nanny share, you'll need to be very organised as well as sensitive to the other family's needs.

Friends and relatives

Not surprisingly, care by a friend or relative is the most common form of childcare in the UK. This is partly because it is usually either free or very cheap. It also gives you the security of knowing that your baby is being cared for by someone you trust implicitly and who genuinely cares for your baby.

Pros

● This is a cheap option.

● Your baby will be looked after in familiar surroundings by someone she knows well.

● This can easily be combined with other kinds of childcare.

● Family and friendship bonds can be strengthened.

Cons

● You may not have as much control over how your baby is fed and cared for as you would with a professional carer.

● Friends and relatives may well have no training in childcare or first aid.

● Knowing your child's carer well can make things difficult if disagreements arise.

● Grandparents may not have as much energy as a younger carer and some can be a little old-fashioned in their approach to childcare.

● Your child may not have as much opportunity to mix with other children.

'Almost as soon as I got pregnant I knew it was going to be my mum who looked after the baby. She's really excited about the idea and I trust her one hundred per cent.'

Genna, legal secretary and eight months pregnant

Making your choice

Once you've researched what is available in your area and decided what kind of childcare you'd like, it's time to set up some appointments. Before you get on the phone, you may find it helpful to jot down your basic requirements. When will you need childcare to start, for example? What's the furthest you are willing to travel? What hours will you need and how much flexibility? How much are your prepared to pay and what qualifications are you looking for? Armed with your list you'll be able to exclude some of your choices without going to the trouble of a visit.

Ideally, you should have a shortlist of at least three nurseries, childminders or nannies to see. If it's a nursery or childminder you are considering, ask them to send you any printed information they may have, plus a copy of the latest Ofsted report. For a nanny, you'll obviously want to see a CV before you meet up. Arrange to meet your shortlisted carers at a time when they'll be caring for children. If you are inviting potential nannies to your home, try to set up appointments for a time in the day when your baby is likely to be awake.

Lots of mums have an instinct for who they feel would be the right person, or people, to look after their baby. It's important to choose carers who share your views on how to look after children, but it's the relationship they'll have with your baby that really counts. Watching your potential carer, or carers, in action with babies or children will give you an idea of just how child-friendly they really are.

Ask yourself:

- Are they warm and responsive?

- Do they watch and listen carefully?

- Are they playful and imaginative?

- Can they chat easily to little ones?

- Are they patient?

- Can they join in with your child's play without taking over?

● Can they spot difficult situations, such as your baby becoming overtired, before they arise?

If you are considering a nursery or childminder for your baby, you'll also want to consider the environment in which she'll be cared for. Is there plenty of clean, modern play equipment, for example? Is the food provided healthy? What procedures are in place in the event of an emergency? Is there plenty of space for outdoor play? Is the environment non-smoking or are there pets? Ask to be shown round every area that your child will use and make sure you see the kitchen and toilets, too. The state of those will tell you volumes about how the place is run.

Once you've made your choice, it's vital that you follow up references. A good carer will be happy to give you contact details for other parents who've used their services. If you haven't already seen an up-to-date Ofsted report, ask to see one now along with registration and insurance certificates.

Don't feel you have to decide in a rush. Your carer will be a very important person in your family's life until your child reaches school age and possibly beyond, so it's important that you feel happy with your decision. If necessary, arrange two or even three visits with your chosen carer to make sure you are completely comfortable with your choice.

> 'When I first met Amina, she took Ellie from me and sat with her on her lap while we chatted. You could see that Ellie was relaxed with her. She's been our childminder for ten months now, and she's like part of the family.'
>
> Ruth, music teacher and mum to Ellie, 22 months

Once you've decided

Once you've made your decision, it time to formalise the arrangement between you and your new carer. Most nurseries and childminders will ask you to sign a pro-forma contract outlining what you will pay and what they will provide in return. You will usually be asked for a retainer fee as well. If you are hiring a childminder, the contract should also cover holiday arrangements (hers and yours) and what happens in the event that she or your child is ill.

If you are hiring a nanny, you will be responsible for drawing up her contract (you can download sample nanny contracts from the internet if you wish). However well you get on with the person you've decided to hire, don't be tempted to leave your arrangement informal. Offer her a proper contract outlining:

● the start date

● salary

● hours of work

● holiday and sick leave entitlement

● notice period

● details of disciplinary procedures.

You may also want to cover any evening or weekend work you'll expect her to do, use of the telephone and car, house rules about friends, smoking and so on, and time off in lieu arrangements. As time goes on, things get forgotten and boundaries start to blur, so it's best to keep things formal from the start.

Whoever your carer is going to be, this is the time to lay out all your expectations about how you want your baby to be cared for. You'll need to make it clear what food, how many naps and how much fresh air you want your baby to have, whether or not she can watch TV, how her behaviour should be managed and so on. Ironically, this is even more important if your baby is going to be cared for by a friend or relative. It's easy for boundaries to be less clear when the relationship isn't as professional and it can be much more difficult to resolve disputes if they arise.

Also remember that, whoever is going to be caring for your baby, this is a two-way contract. In return for the love, time and attention your carer shows your baby, you need to reciprocate by dropping off and picking up your baby at the agreed times, not taking advantage in any way and, where appropriate, paying them on time.

Help with the cost

Childcare can make a huge dent in your family budget, especially if you are planning to hire a nanny or use a private nursery. Luckily, there is help available. Nine out of ten families are entitled to financial help through the tax credits system, and the Working Tax Credit contains a childcare element that can be offset against your childcare costs. In order to be eligible, your carer needs to be registered with Ofsted. You and your partner also need to work at least 16 hours a week each (if you are a lone parent you also need to work at least 16 hours a week).

If you are an employee, it's worth checking your contract, too. More and more employers are waking up to the fact that it pays to keep parents on their payroll and so offer extra childcare benefits to their employees. Unless you are lucky enough to work for a company that provides on-site childcare, this usually takes the form of vouchers that can be used to pay for any registered or approved childcare. One big advantage of these is that they are deducted from your pre-tax income, which means your tax liability is smaller. So, as well as having subsidised childcare, you also get to pay less tax.

If you are hiring a nanny, another good way to cut costs is to set up a nanny share. This works well for lots of families, particularly those who only have one child. Often the nanny will look after all the children in alternate homes, but sometimes one family is happy to host the nanny and children in their home. If you decide to go down the nanny-share route, it's best to have a proper contract and keep your arrangements formal. This will make things clear not just between yourselves and your nanny, but also with the other family. It's also sensible to set up regular times to get together and talk about how things are going generally.

> *'Martin and I are both earning, but we still get around £50 a month in tax credits. It's not much, but it helps to keep Natasha in nappies!'*
>
> Hilary, retail buyer and mum to Natasha, 15 months

Childcare for older children

If you are returning to work after several years at home, you'll have a few more childcare options open to you. You are also likely to know other parents with children under five, too, which will make your search easier.

If your children are approaching school age and you have a spare room in your house, you could consider hiring an au pair. Au pairs are usually young, single women who come to the UK to learn English. In return for board, lodging and a small wage, they will help out with childcare and housework. Au pairs are generally inexperienced and unqualified and, as such, shouldn't be given sole responsibility for babies and toddlers. The exception to this is, possibly, if you work from home and can be on hand to tackle any crises.

From the age of three your child is also entitled to a free part-time place in an Ofsted-registered early-learning setting. This could be a playgroup, school nursery, or a local authority or private nursery. There is a huge amount of competition for these places, so do make sure you start your search early and get your child's name down for your chosen setting well ahead of the time you plan to return to work.

SUMMARY OF CHAPTER 5

- Good childcare can be hard to come by, so start your search early.
- Personal recommendations are useful, but do check out all the options available in your area.
- Arrange to see potential carers while they are caring for children or when your own baby is around so that you can see how well they interact with and care for children.
- Take time over your decision and meet with your chosen carer several times beforehand if necessary.
- Always follow up references and read Ofsted reports.
- Always have a contract and put things on to a formal footing from the start to avoid confusion and disagreements later on.
- If a friend or relative is going be caring for your baby, make it clear how you expect them to care for your baby from the beginning – again, this will help to avoid any disagreements.
- Make sure you find out what help is available with the cost of childcare, whether it's tax credits, help from your employer or sharing a nanny.
- Au pairs and early-learning settings offer handy childcare solutions for older children.

CHAPTER 6

Job Options:
New Ways to Work

You are excited about going back to work, using your skills and being part of a team again, but while you are ready to take on the demands of a working mum, you also know that your appetite for long hours, work trips abroad and report writing in your spare time has vanished along with your flat stomach. You want – and need – a more family-friendly work environment. So what are your options?

Flexible working is a solution that works for many mums. And while changing and/or reducing your hours could have a knock-on effect on your family's income, and possibly on your career, too, this may help you achieve the work/life balance you are looking for. But how easy is it to achieve? The good news is that under recent legislation employers are now legally required to consider a request for flexible working conditions. But, of course, this doesn't mean your boss has to say yes. If opportunities for flexible working arrangements don't already exist in your company, you'll need to negotiate your way forward.

Alternatively, you may consider a more radical solution such as changing direction altogether. Many women see their maternity leave as an opportunity to rethink their career and explore new ways of working. This may involve going freelance, for example, setting up your own business, retraining or taking a career break.

Whatever route you decide to go down, it's also worth bearing in mind that finding a happy balance between work and family life doesn't have to be your sole responsibility. Flexible working may be easier for your partner to achieve, for example, and changing his work patterns could make life easier for both of you.

Flexible working

Flexible working is often the best option for mums balancing work and children. Here are some of the more common types of flexi work.

Full-time flexible hours

Full-time flexibility means you continue with your normal full-time hours, and full-time salary, but you spread them across the week depending on your needs. This has lots of benefits: you keep your salary, but arrange your hours to fit in with your home life. Normally, flexi workers are expected to work a number of core hours – for example 10am to 4pm. The rest of the working day is 'flexible'. This means either side of these core hours you can choose the number of hours you work, as long you work your agreed total daily, weekly or monthly hours. Simply not having to be in the office at nine in the morning can take much of the stress out of getting your child to the childminder, nursery or school. Some schemes also allow workers to put in extra hours one day, and take time off the next – so if you need time to take your child to the doctor or dentist you don't need to use up precious annual leave.

Part-time hours

Working part time is the most popular choice for mothers with young children – and it's easy to see why. Part-time hours allow you to enjoy the benefits of working and being a mum. It can, however, be very difficult finding reasonably paid and satisfying part-time work. And many mums in part-time work feel they are expected to do five days' work in less time, particularly when they work four days. Others encounter prejudice, particularly the higher up they go. Often part-timers aren't considered as full members of the team, which is reflected in the relatively small number of part-timers in senior positions. All this is in spite of the fact that recent research has shown that part-timers are better organised, more motivated, more productive, happier in their jobs and less likely to call in sick.

> *'Working part time was the best choice I ever made. We can't afford holidays abroad any more, and I don't think I've done my long-term promotion prospects any favours, but for now both these sacrifices were worth making.'*
>
> Catherine, accountant and mum to Alice, four, and Ben, six

Job sharing

This is when two people fill one job with each person having a permanent, part-time post, splitting hours, salary, holiday and benefits. One person might do mornings, another afternoons; or one do Monday and Tuesday, and the other Wednesday, Thursday, Friday. This is a great option for working parents as salary and promotion prospects remain intact. It's also a good option for employers – two great minds on the job, rather than just one. And while you are very dependent on your job-sharer for ensuring the arrangement works well, on the upside you get to share problems.

Term-time/school-hours working

Both of these are great arrangements once your child is at school, as finding cover after school or for school holidays can be a nightmare. If you work school hours only, you can drop off and pick up your child from school. With term-time working, instead of having the typical four to six weeks' annual holiday, you have an extra seven to nine weeks' unpaid leave. This means taking a drop in salary (usually averaged out over the year) but gives you the chance to work during term time and spend the school holidays with your child. Many employers may, however, be reluctant to find cover during your absences – although in industries where there are seasonal peaks and troughs, term-time working could be seen as an advantage.

> *'Local councils are great places to work if you are looking for flexible hours. I changed jobs when Fran was born and although in some ways I preferred the faster pace of the corporate world, I've found the public service environment is very supportive towards mothers.'*
>
> Gael, environmental health officer and mum to Fran, three

Working from home

Home working – also known as tele-working, or remote working – can make a big difference. Although it would be impossible to care full time for your child and work effectively, working from home can make the organisation and management of childcare much easier and less stressful. You also have greater flexibility to cope with emergencies, and if you'd otherwise have a long commute, you also get to swap travelling time for family time. It's worth bearing in mind, however, that working from home isn't necessarily the dream option you might imagine. While there's no commuting, no office politics and no meetings, you may feel isolated and out of the loop, especially as you have no work colleagues on hand to bounce ideas off, and creating a clear distinction between work and home life can be more difficult. You also need to be able to manage your time effectively and say no to interruptions – friends dropping by, domestic chores staring you in the face, the biscuit tin!

> *'I love the flexibility of working from home – but it can get lonely. Once my children are at secondary school and I'm not needed for pick-ups and drop-offs, I'll really miss the playground gossip.'*
>
> Miriam, freelance journalist and mum to Rosie, seven, and Tom, five

How to negotiate new hours

Once you've decided that flexible working is the best arrangement for you, what next? Although employers are legally obliged to take requests for flexible working seriously, they don't have to agree. So how can you persuade yours?

Firstly, you need to check that you qualify for the right to request flexible working. Currently, you must have a child under six years (or under 18 if the child receives Disability Living Allowance), although this may soon be extended to older children too. You must also make the request no later than two weeks before the child's sixth (or 18th) birthday and have worked for your employer for at least 26 weeks when you make the request.

Next, think about your strategy. Bear in mind that you and your boss probably want the same thing – for you, an experienced employee, to stay with the organisation. But you still need to have a plan that will work not only for you, but also for your boss. If your company doesn't already offer a flexible package, you'll need to convince them that it's not going to disadvantage the business – or cause hassle for your fellow employees. Remember that your employer will take a while to process your request, so try to get it in at least eight weeks before you return to work.

One obvious argument in your favour is that having a better work/life balance can help you focus more clearly and productively on your work. But also, it may be worth pointing out that organisations that are able to offer flexible working packages often have an advantage when recruiting new staff; and experienced staff are less likely to leave – which can cut the costs of training, recruitment and lost productivity.

- **Decide what you want:** make sure you are clear about your request – are you looking for flexible hours, fewer hours, term-time work, an option to work from home? Aim high – this will give you room to negotiate, and leave you with a deal that's still better than your current one.

- **Get advice:** it might be worth speaking to your company's human resources department, and if you belong to a trade union you could ask for a meeting with your local representative. If they have advised staff on similar issues before, they might have some useful advice. And they can put you in contact with staff who have successfully negotiated flexible working hours.

- **Make your case:** legally, your request must be made in writing. The easiest way to do this is to use the 'Flexible working application form' which can be downloaded from the government website (www.berr.gov.uk/publications). Think about your employer's specific concerns and likely objections – and how you might be able to overcome these. Then set out clearly and concisely what you are looking for, and the benefits to you and your organisation. Your employer must then arrange a meeting to consider your request within 28 days of receiving your request.

- **On the day:** during the meeting with your boss, remember to thank him or her for considering your ideas. Stay calm and try not to get emotional – even if the answer is no, you will have to continue working together.

- **Following your meeting:** your employer must give you a decision in writing within 14 days. A request can only be turned down for one or more permitted reasons, and these need to be stated by your employer. If this does happen, you then have 14 days to appeal, in writing. If your appeal is not upheld, and you want to take matters further, you may consider going to an employment tribunal. In this case, you will need to seek the help of a solicitor or your trade union. For further advice, see Sources of Further Information (page 165).

Making your workplace family friendly

Working for a family-friendly employer – one that offers benefits such as flexible working, childcare help, job-share schemes and home working – can make a huge difference to your life, as an employee and a parent.

Some companies, however, are still stuck in the dark ages – although getting them to review their policies and work culture may be simpler than you think. After all, there's lots of research to show that family-friendly working practices can improve productivity and help companies hang on to skilled staff. Work sectors that still follow the old nine-to-five model, such as the sciences and engineering, find it very difficult to attract women and have lots of staff shortages as a result.

So, before you ditch your job in despair, why not try to change attitudes where you work instead? Here are some ideas as to what you could do.

- **Set up a parents' group:** there's greater strength in numbers, and together you can come up with workable ways of potentially improving the environment for other employees who are parents, too. Talk to your manager about what you hope to achieve and why it's important. Help them understand that you see discussion as a way of improving morale and productivity.

- **Find positive examples:** look in the trade press, business sections of daily newspapers and profiles of big companies for examples where family-friendly policies are working to the benefit of everyone. Use them as evidence that achieving your purpose will be good all round.

- **Put together a proposal:** find out the best person to talk to and ask how they want to receive your proposal for change – in writing, perhaps, or via a presentation. When preparing your proposal, bear in mind that a good proposal does the following.

  - Lays out the problems clearly, giving concrete examples.

  - Suggests realistic changes that could be made to solve these problems.

- Outlines the benefits this will bring to your employer as well as employees.

The trick is to be positive and constructive rather than negative and critical. Be prepared to give way on some points, but stick to your guns over things that really matter. And do follow it up if you don't hear back promptly.

● **Be optimistic:** no one wants to work alongside a colleague who complains all the time. Instead, try to be positive, and focus on finding strategies that will make a difference. You may even get colleagues without children on board, too – after all, no one enjoys a work environment where it's frowned on if they leave on time, and there's no flexibility to deal with everyday emergencies.

> *'We have a parents' group at work and some of us have worked with the human resources department to create a booklet for women going off on maternity leave. I think new mums feel better supported now, and are more likely to come back to work.'*
>
> Ann-Marie, production supervisor and mum to Jack, ten, Isla, seven, and Ethan, three

New directions

If your present job can't offer you the flexibility you are looking for, or you want to leave for other reasons, depending on your skills, finances and long-term plans, there are other choices available to you.

Going freelance

Being your own boss has lots of benefits, especially for mums. Besides giving you the flexibility of hours to fit your work in with parenting, it may also give you the freedom to select who you work with, when and where. If the nature of your job allows you to go freelance, you may want to try it out first before taking the plunge. Jobs that lend themselves to freelance work include those in PR, marketing, photography, design, journalism, IT, hair and beauty, and translating. A sensible first step may be to negotiate fewer hours in your present job while you see whether freelancing can work for you. Bear in mind, however, that childcare could still be an issue – although deadlines may be flexible up to a point, you may not always be able to guarantee that you can get a job done during napping or nursery hours.

Setting up a business

Becoming a mum and needing to rethink your work/life balance may be just the motivation you need to get that germ of a business idea up and running. Do think carefully, however, about how the business will fit into your life – realistically, can you start a new venture and a new family at the same time? Chances are you will still need childcare, but you could be home-based, which will take a lot of the stress out of working for yourself. Think also about whether you have the right temperament for starting and running your own business. Do you have the confidence to take calculated risks? Are you willing to market yourself and your business? Can you raise the money to fund your project? If you think you have what it takes, now could be the best time ever to give it a go. You can find out more about setting up your own business at www.businesslink.gov.uk.

'Once my youngest started school I was desperate to start work again. Then I saw an article about setting up your own local advertising magazine – and knew it was what I wanted to do. It's been hard work – I'm often back at my desk long after the children have gone to bed. But I'm really thriving on the challenge.'

Pippa, magazine publisher
and mum to Jonah, 12, Cameron, 11, and Finley, five

Retraining

If you've always wanted to do something different, or know that long term your present job and family life won't mix, this might be a good time to retrain. It doesn't necessarily have to be expensive. Although giving up work will mean the loss of your income, some professions – those with a shortage of skilled workers, such as teaching, nursing and others professions in the health service – may offer payment while you train. Otherwise it may be worth looking at part-time training, distance learning and online courses, which may allow you to continue working in some capacity. Of course, there is still the need for childcare, although if the hours aren't too demanding, you may find family or friends who can help out. If retraining is something you are passionate about, it's worth taking a long-term view – investing in yourself now can reap benefits for everyone in the family.

'I started as a part-time classroom assistant when my youngest, Elly, was at nursery school. Then I did a post-grad teacher-training course, and now I'm a fully qualified teacher. It's tough, but I love it. And there's never a problem with childcare over school holidays.'

Lily, former NHS radiographer, now primary school teacher and mum to Max, nine, and Elly, six

Taking a career break

If managing work and motherhood makes you miserable, you may feel your only choice is to leave work altogether. If you think you might want to return at a later date, try to keep up your skills – do some relevant voluntary work, for example, or look for suitable adult education classes. Having ongoing contact with the working world in some capacity will not only give you something to put on your CV when you do take the plunge and return to work, but also help remind you of your capabilities and potential value as an employee.

SUMMARY OF CHAPTER 6

- Working flexible hours is a solution for many mums looking for a better work/life balance. Flexible working offers many options.
- Although you have a legal right to request flexible working, you employer doesn't have to agree to it.
- To apply for flexible working you need to make a written request.
- Other work options include working for yourself, retraining or taking a career break.

CHAPTER 7

Back to Work: Get Ready, Get Set

When you've had many months at home, safe and snug in your new world with your new baby, the thought of venturing back to work and leaving your child with another person may be something you'd rather not think about. But while your maternity leave is precious, it makes sense to use the time to think ahead about the challenges you'll face when you return to work, as getting prepared now will help to reduce the inevitable practical and emotional stresses.

Getting your baby into a routine

Babies love routine. And once you are back at work and your baby is in childcare, your mornings and evenings will be a whole lot easier if your baby already has a good routine. He'll also be more settled if he can follow the same routine while he's with his carer as he does when he's with you at the weekends.

Your baby's routine needn't be timetabled to the minute, but, by the time you return to work, he should certainly have regular naps, mealtimes and, most important of all, a set bedtime. Establishing a regular bedtime will not only help your baby to sleep more soundly, it also allows you to plan the rest of his day more easily. If he goes to sleep at about 7pm, for example, you can then schedule in one or two naps (afternoon naps shouldn't be too close to bedtime) and slot his mealtimes around these.

To some extent you'll need to be guided by your baby's own natural rhythms. Do remember, though, that your baby is just one member of your family and it's perfectly reasonable to nudge his routine slightly here and there so that it fits in better with yours.

Ready for childcare

Handing your baby over to a childcarer for the first time is an emotional moment for every mother and certainly not something you'll want to be doing on your first day back at work. Introducing him to childcare gradually in the month or so before you return will be far kinder to you both.

Make a note of your baby's routine so that your carer can keep to the same pattern. The less disruption your baby has to cope with, the faster he'll settle. It's a good idea to stay with your baby and his carer for the first couple of times, too. Babies need time to warm to strangers, and seeing you chatting, relaxing and interacting with his new carer (or carers) will help him to relax, too. Once your baby seems settled, it's time to bite the bullet and leave him alone with his carer. A couple of hours is plenty to begin with, building up to a whole day just before you return to work.

> *'I planned to do lots of jobs around the house when Mae went to nursery for the first time. I didn't do a thing. I just moped around wondering if she was OK. When it was time to pick her up, I couldn't get there quickly enough.'*
>
> Catherine, accountant and mum to Mae, 19 months, and George, seven weeks

Think about emergency childcare

You may have found the most perfect childcarer in the world but, like you, they are only human and may not be able to work occasionally due to illness and other problems. It is sensible, therefore, to think about what will happen in this situation before you go back to work. This will avoid desperate early morning phone calls to friends and family to find someone who can look after your baby. Many mums find the alternative –

phoning work to say you can't come in because of childcare problems – just as difficult.

If you've decided to take your baby to a nursery, you probably won't have this problem as nursery staff are usually covered for sickness and leave. On the other side of the coin, nurseries are often less willing to take children who are under the weather than carers who look after children in the home.

If you are lucky, you may have friends or relatives who are happy to take your baby whenever your childcare arrangements break down. Alternatively, you could talk to your carer to see if they know any other reliable carers who would be prepared to look after your baby occasionally.

Also talk to your partner about who will take time off in the event that your child is ill or your carer is not available. Don't assume that it will automatically be you, and make sure he doesn't either. It makes no sense for you to use up all your annual leave covering childcare emergencies, leaving little for spending time together as a family.

You also have other options besides using your annual leave. Provided you are employees, both you and your partner are entitled to parental leave, which allows each parent 13 weeks of unpaid leave before their child's fifth birthday. You are also entitled to something called 'time off for dependants'. This covers emergencies involving someone who depends on you, including a breakdown in childcare arrangements or childhood illness. The leave may not be paid – this is at your employer's discretion – but it does allow you as much time as you need to sort the emergency out.

Breastfeeding and work

It can feel that, no sooner have you mastered breastfeeding, than it's time to start thinking about expressing and bottles so that you can return to work. Of course, if you are lucky enough to work from home – or if you work part time and flexibly – you may be able to continue breastfeeding more or less as normal. Even if you are working full days, it's perfectly possible to continue feeding your baby in the mornings and evenings as well as at weekends.

The thought of continuing breastfeeding while working can be a daunting prospect, and some mums choose to wean their babies at this point. However, while combining breastfeeding and work takes some organisation, it's definitely possible and does have some huge advantages.

For a start it's a great way to keep the bond between you and your baby strong even though you are separated for long periods. There's nothing quite as wonderful as enjoying a quiet bedtime breastfeed with your baby after a frazzled day at work. You'll also have the satisfaction of knowing that your baby is still getting all the benefits that breastmilk provides. Another important benefit is that breastfed babies tend to have fewer chest infections and tummy upsets, which is great for your baby and means less disruption at work for you.

If you plan to continue breastfeeding, you have two options: you can either express your own milk or you can start combining formula and breastmilk – what's known as mixed feeding. You'll need to start this process a month or so before you return to work. If you plan to introduce formula, this will give your body time to adjust to making less milk. If you are expressing, it will give you plenty of time to build up your technique and make sure you are producing enough milk. It will also mean you have a healthy supply of breastmilk in your freezer by the time you go back to work. If you are not sure where to start, the National Childbirth Trust produces a useful leaflet called *Breastfeeding: how to express and store your milk* (£2.50) – visit their website at www.nctsales.co.uk or phone 0870 112 1120.

Whether you have decided to express or to combine breastmilk and formula, you'll need to introduce your baby to a bottle. This may sound simple, but it's amazing how unco-operative a happily breastfeeding baby can be when an alien rubber teat is stuck in his mouth. Of course, you may find your baby takes to it like duck to water, but if he doesn't, try some of the following:

- **Experiment with different feeding positions:** some mums find that laying their baby on their lap, away from their breasts, helps.

- **Ask a friend, relative or your partner:** go out for an hour or so and ask someone else to try your baby with a bottle while you are out.

- **Ask your childcarer:** if you are already having short, introductory sessions with your childcarer, ask her to give your baby a bottle.

- **Experiment with different teats:** some babies prefer one type over another.

- **Try a soft-spouted beaker:** if your baby is six months old or more, this may do the trick.

- **Try not to fret:** it may take a little perseverance, but your baby will take a bottle or beaker in the end.

> *'Elsie still wasn't taking a bottle when I went back to work, and I was in a complete state about it. My childminder, who's very experienced, told me not to worry, and sure enough Elsie was taking a bottle from her within a few days.'*
>
> Martine, writer and mum to Elsie, ten, and Rose, six

Reconnecting with work

If you are planning to return to work on the date agreed with your employer, you can in theory simply turn up on the day. In practice, this obviously isn't a good idea – you may well walk in to find no desk waiting for you! If you want to return sooner than the agreed date, you'll need to give your employer eight weeks' notice. If you want to go back later, you need to tell your employer at least eight weeks before your *original* return date.

It makes a lot of sense to plan your return to work with your employer. This will help them to organise things properly at their end, and it will also give you the opportunity to negotiate a new work pattern if you wish. You may wish to request flexible working, for example (see page 58). Remember that your employer will take a while to process your request, so try to get it in at least eight weeks before you return.

The amount of maternity leave you take has important implications for your job. If you return to work after taking 26 weeks' ordinary maternity leave only, you can walk straight back into your old job. However, if you take any more than this, your employer can offer you a different job, provided it's at the same level of responsibility and has the same terms and conditions.

It's also important to tell your employer if you are still going to be breastfeeding when you return, as breastfeeding mums have different rights to mums who are bottle-feeding. For a start, your employer must carry out an assessment to identify any health and safety risks to you and your baby. They also have to provide suitable rest facilities for you. If you are planning to express breastmilk at work, you should be provided with a private place to express and a fridge to store your milk in.

> *'I went away for the weekend about three weeks before I started work, leaving Alex to look after Charlie on his own. It threw him in at the deep end, but he loved every minute of it and coped fantastically.'*
>
> Louise, human resources manager and
> mum to Charlie, 13 months

When you've had a long break

Returning to work after a career break is rather different to stepping back into the same job with the same organisation. When you haven't seen the inside of a workplace for some years, it's natural to feel rather out of touch and lacking in confidence. In fact, you probably have more going for you than you imagine.

Don't feel you have to apologise for taking a break for a start – it's not as though you have been sitting around filing your nails. You have been doing the important and challenging job of raising children and it's vital not to underestimate the new skills you have acquired – there's nothing like being a mother to hone your organisational and time-management skills. Any voluntary work you may have done, such as helping with the running of your child's playgroup, will also give your CV a boost. Jobs like this can really broaden and strengthen your experience and make you attractive to potential employers.

If returning to work feels like a mammoth task and you are wondering where to start, try breaking the process down into manageable chunks.

- **Clarify your goals:** sit down with a piece of paper and write down where and how you'd like to be working in a year's time. How much do you want to earn? Do you want a part-time job or to work flexibly? What kind of work would you like to do? What kind of employer would you like to work for? Once you are clear about the kind of work you want to do, you'll find it easier to identify the steps you need to take to get there.

- **Identify any skills gaps:** although you will have developed new skills since you last worked, you may be lacking others needed to get you where you want. If your IT skills are out of date, you may want to enrol on a computer course at a local college. Some colleges do general courses for women 'returners', which concentrate on things like writing an application and how to do a good interview. Alternatively, try to get a few days' work experience in your chosen field – it's a great way to dip your toe in the water and give your confidence a boost.

- **Spruce up your CV:** you may prefer to do a skills-based CV that focuses on your skills rather than the jobs you have held. Check out the internet, too: there are plenty of websites that show you how to put a good CV together.

- **Spring-clean your wardrobe:** if you are going to an interview, it's important to look professional. If your wardrobe is full of comfy, practical tops and bottoms, it's time to hit the shops and treat yourself to a couple of fabulous work outfits.

- **Start networking:** this isn't just for high-powered businesswomen. All that's needed is a few phone calls to family, friends and acquaintances to explain that you are hoping to return to work and asking if they know anyone who can help. You'll be amazed how quickly useful contacts come along once you start to put feelers out. There are also more formal networks you can explore – the Women Returners Network (www.women-returners.co.uk) is a great place to start.

- **Take the plunge:** at some point you'll need to get serious about finding work. Look in the jobs pages, phone up the human resources sections of organisations you'd like to work for and send your CV to prospective employers. Don't forget to ask about unpaid work experience, too. Stay positive and be persistent and you will undoubtedly succeed in the end.

SUMMARY OF CHAPTER 7

- Work on getting your baby into a simple routine before you return, and remember to share it with your childcarer.
- Introduce your baby to childcare gradually – go with him for the first couple of times.
- Plan for childcare emergencies, such as your child or childcarer being ill.
- Start introducing your baby to bottles of formula or expressed breastmilk at least a month before you return.
- Reconnect with work – if you are planning to renegotiate your hours, make sure you get in touch at least two months before you go back.
- If you've had a long break from work, spruce up your CV and your wardrobe and get networking!

CHAPTER 8

Life at Work: The First Few Weeks

The first few weeks back at work will leave you exhausted. You now have another important person in your life to consider, as well as less time to manage your home and to spend on yourself and your partner. For your baby, no amount of extra household income will substitute for a relaxed and happy home environment, free of stress and conflict. So it's important that you and your partner are supportive of each other and that you make time to look after yourself.

Leaving your baby

When the day comes for you to say goodbye and set off for work, you need to be prepared for some upset, especially if you haven't already done a try-out with your carer. If your baby is going through separation anxiety, she's particularly likely to be clingy. Put yourself in her place for a moment, and it's easy to see why: she has no idea when, or even if, you are going to return. Trying to keep the situation happy and calm, even if you feel in complete turmoil, will reassure her. Avoid long goodbyes. Give her a hug, kiss her goodbye, and then go without any fuss. Try not to worry too much if she cries as you leave. This is very normal and, as any experienced childcarer will tell you, she'll soon settle down once you are out of sight.

You may find that your baby is very soon happily waving you goodbye through the sitting room or nursery window. Some babies, however, will carry on being fretful when they are left, in which case you may want to peep back through the window after a few minutes to be reassured that she's fine.

Picking your baby up in the evening will be the first of many lovely reunions at the end of the working day. Again, try to be matter of fact and calm. You may feel very emotional, but your baby will be unsettled by any unusual strength of feeling, and is likely to burst into tears as well. Some mums also find that their babies are 'difficult' at the end of the day. This is entirely normal: she's just checking that you still love her by demanding lots of attention.

Meanwhile, building a good relationship and treating your baby's carer as a partner will help motivate her to keep up good standards of care. Helping to tidy up at the end of the day, chatting about what's happened, and saying thank you for the day's work will always be appreciated. If any problems come up and you feel too tired or rushed to deal with them there and then, make sure you set up a time to thrash them out within the next few days. When problems and issues are left to fester, there's always the risk that they will escalate.

> *'I felt awful leaving Audrey, but I'd already arranged with the nursery that I would call to see how she was as soon as I got into work. Of course, she was fine and she was all smiles when I picked her up.'*
>
> Jess, fashion designer and mum to Audrey, 20 months

Your first day

As with just about everything else to do with being a working mother, the key to surviving your first day at work is good planning. Chances are your little one will sense that you have a big day ahead and will have a particularly wakeful night (welcome to the life of a working mum!), so arrange for your partner to get up with your baby during the night if necessary. Pack your workbag and lay out your work clothes, then enjoy a relaxing evening and an early night.

Having spent months, if not years, at home with your baby, your first day at work is bound to feel a little strange. While you have been through the life-transforming experience of having a baby and becoming a mother, life for your work colleagues will probably have continued much the same as usual. So don't feel too disappointed if their welcome seems a little understated or if the monthly sales targets no longer seem as gripping as they once did.

It's bound to be an emotional day, too. Commuting and spending a whole day away from your baby is quite a different matter to leaving her with a carer for a few hours while you potter about at home. Do remember to take some baby photos with you – your colleagues will want to see them in any case, and you'll be able to give yourself a regular fix of her gummy smile throughout the day. You can also allow yourself at least one phone call to your childcarer to make sure she's OK.

If you are still breastfeeding, be prepared to have uncomfortably full breasts for a few days. Wear breastpads and make sure you pack some extras, plus a clean bra and top, to keep in your desk drawer or locker.

Be kind to yourself. Going back to work after having a baby is a big step. It's bound to take you a little while to re-adapt to working life and to get used to being without your baby. Rather than getting stuck right into a meaty work project, it's probably more helpful to see your first day as a 'settling back in' day. Your colleagues won't have huge expectations of you in any case – they've already managed to do without you for quite some time and a couple more days won't matter. Don't be too ambitious on your first day.

- **Make sure you have everything you need:** order new stationery, make sure your workstation is comfortable and that you still know how to work the photocopier.

- **Have a catch-up with your manager:** ask him or her about any important things you may have missed while you were away as well as what's coming up, and make sure there are no outstanding personnel issues.

- **Go round and talk to everyone about your baby:** you'll be amazed how quickly people start glazing over at the mention of your precious bundle, but on your first day people will be dying to see your baby photos and hear all your news, so go for it!

- **Phone up all your contacts to say you are back:** make a list of everyone you need to call, get on the phone and enjoy leisurely catch-ups with all your most important people.

- **Take a proper lunch hour and enjoy it:** wander round the shops, treat yourself to a tasty lunch or just sit in the park and enjoy the feeling of freedom.

At the end of the day, you'll probably need to leave promptly in order to pick up your baby. When you are used to being able to spend an extra 15 minutes at the end of the day to finish whatever you are working on, this can come as quite a shock to the system. From now on, you simply have to walk out as soon as the working day ends. This is something that you (and your colleagues) will become used to in time. If you find it a problem in the long term, you'll need to think about extending your childcare hours or arranging for your partner to do more pick-ups so that your can have more flexibility.

> *'My first day back at work was one of the worst of my life. I had a cold and so did Arthur and neither of us had had a wink of sleep. I remember sitting on a freezing cold bus going into town thinking, "What am I doing?"'*
>
> Jane, production editor and mum to Arthur, 23 months

Expressing at work

As many mums discover, expressing at work sometimes requires a certain amount of grit and determination. You may find that your employer is bemused or even negative about the idea of you expressing at work. In fact, supporting you to express is very much in their interests: one US study found that breastfeeding mothers are three times less likely to take time off work for baby illnesses than mothers who bottle-feed their babies.

Ideally, your employer should provide a clean, warm, private room, preferably with an electrical socket and a fridge where breastmilk can be stored safely. Sadly, in practice you are more likely to find yourself expressing in the ladies and wedging your bottle bag in between the sandwich boxes in the general office fridge.

Try not to let this put you off. Expressing gives you a few precious moments each day when you can forget all about work and just think about your gorgeous baby. It also gives you the satisfaction of knowing that you are doing your very best for her. If you really can't face expressing in the ladies, you may like to consider getting together with other breastfeeding mums and lobbying for a dedicated, private area for expressing.

Try to express at the same time every day to avoid your breasts becoming overfull, and make sure you arrange meetings and work-related trips around your expressing routine. Looking at pictures of your baby will help your milk to let down. Once you've expressed, your pump will need a quick rinse under the tap and your milk should go straight into a fridge. It's a good idea to transfer the milk to an insulated bottle bag for the journey home.

'I expressed at work for four months. It all felt like a bit of a faff at first, but I quickly got into a routine and actually it was a great excuse to have a few quiet moments to myself in the middle of the day.'

Mandy, public information officer and mum to Maisie, two

Sleep (or lack of it)

You probably felt exhausted while you were on maternity leave, but at least you could have the occasional lie in or nap. Now you are working again, it doesn't matter how wakeful your baby has been during the night, you are still expected to turn up for work and act professionally while you are there.

Lots of mums don't like the idea of sleep training – until they go back to work! The fact is that being utterly exhausted is no good for you or for your baby. Most babies are able to sleep through the night from around six months, but some just need a little encouragement to do so.

The first trick is to make sure that your baby has a really good bedtime routine. Having, for example, her supper, bath, book and bed in the same order and the same time every night signals to your baby that this is the time for sleep. If she cries when you leave her, go back and comfort her with a few words or a pat, but don't take her out of her cot. Go back as many times as it takes to settle her and she will gradually get the idea that this is not the time for cuddles or playing with mummy, but for sleep.

Dragging yourself through a working day when you've been up since five really is one of the worst feelings in the world. You feel lethargic, get irritable over the slightest thing and can't concentrate to save your life. One of the biggest helps – if at all possible – is to get a catnap at lunchtime. Anywhere will do – a staff room, storage cupboard, park, car (if your drive to work) or, if you are lucky enough to have your own office, under your desk. Just set the alarm on your mobile and treat yourself to a luxurious 20-minute nap. You may like to try these other survival tips, too.

- **Drink a cup of coffee:** a shot of caffeine can help if you've got a boring meeting coming up.

- **March out of the office:** walk briskly round the block taking deep breaths as you go. This can help if you are falling asleep at your desk.

- **Plan your day:** schedule more demanding tasks for the morning and save easier jobs for your mid-afternoon slump.

- **Go to bed early:** even at the same time as your baby. This may seem a bit extreme, but just think how amazing it will be to feel fresh and on top of things at work the next day.

Looking after yourself

Mothers are notoriously bad at taking care of themselves, but during your first few weeks back at work it's essential that you do. Otherwise you will become frazzled and exhausted, and may start to feel that you are not coping either at home or at work. Here are some suggestions to help make your working days easier.

- **Eat healthily:** take in healthy sandwiches, soup or salads rather than always opting for the delights of your local sandwich bar.

- **Snack healthily:** avoid the traditional caffeine and sugar break as this will only leave you feeling worse later on. Go for a banana, a handful of almonds or a cereal bar, instead.

- **Go out:** arrange to meet friends for lunch occasionally or go for an evening out straight after work.

- **Get fit:** use your lunch hour to do an exercise class or, if your workplace offers a discount at a local gym, sign up.

- **Relax:** build relaxation into your working day, even if it's just ten minutes reading a book in the park during your lunch hour or five minutes' deep breathing at your desk.

- **Work from home:** ask your manager if this can be arranged occasionally. It's good to get a break from the daily commute.

- **Learn when to ask for help:** there's no merit in struggling with a problem on your own, and people are usually flattered to be asked.

- **Don't ignore stress:** if you are feeling stressed, do something about it. Renegotiate your workload with your manager or organise to have a day off soon to give yourself some breathing space.

> *'I treat myself to a posh coffee and a sticky Danish pastry on my way to work each Monday. It's only a small thing, but it puts a smile on my face and gets my week off to a good start.'*
>
> Wendy, arts administrator and mum to William, five, and Alex, 11 months

SUMMARY OF CHAPTER 8

- Try to keep your goodbyes to your baby short and cheery.
- Go easy on yourself on your first day – no one will expect you to get up to speed immediately.
- If you are expressing milk, try to do so at the same time every day.
- Looking at photos of your baby will help your milk to flow.
- If your baby is wakeful at night, encourage her to sleep by setting up a regular bedtime routine.
- If you feel exhausted at work, try to catnap or go for a brisk walk round the block.
- Look after yourself – getting some exercise, eating well and making time for relaxation will help to stop you feeling exhausted and overwhelmed.

CHAPTER 9

You and Your Partner: Sharing the Load

Having a baby transforms your life. Everything is different – not just your daily routines and your social life, but your relationship, too. And for many parents, the first year after birth – especially once you are back at work – can be among the rockiest. Both you and your partner are shattered and have little time at the end of the day for each other. There are fewer and fewer occasions when you are alone together and life revolves around your baby's needs, which can't be postponed. Inevitably, with less time to talk and feel close, issues like who empties the bins or gets up in the night for the baby can create conflict. Both of you need more love and attention, but instead resentment can build.

If you and your partner start to grow apart during these early months, it can become increasingly hard to get your relationship back on track in the years that follow. But if you work hard to keep your relationship strong, your whole family will be strong – you'll both be better parents, life will be more peaceful and everyone will have more fun. The key lies in sharing childcare and household chores, making time for each other, and continuing to talk and listen.

If you are a single parent, there is, of course, no one to argue with about those socks that never get put in the laundry basket, or whose turn it is to puree the carrots. Instead, it's your friends and family you'll turn to when you need a break from childcare, help getting the shopping in or just someone to share your worries with.

Doing it all

It's a trap that's easy to fall into – managing a job and then rushing home to manage the house and care for your child, too. According to the National Statistics Office, women do roughly two-thirds of all housework in the UK. But shouldering most of the chores on top of holding down a job will not only leave you exhausted, but also increasingly resentful, and ultimately unable to feel close and loving towards your partner because you feel neither cared for nor supported by him.

Looking after children and running a house can be a full-time job in itself. Domestic chores demand time and energy, even if you are happy to get by with the bare minimum. But this is your family home, so it makes sense that both of you take responsibility for all the demands that it entails. Before discussing this, think about the language you use. Rather than talking about how your partner can 'help' you with the household responsibilities, talk about 'sharing' them instead.

Caring for your child

Everyone benefits – you, your partner and your child – if you're both involved in childcare.

- **Start as you mean to go on:** share the day-to-day care of your baby from the very start. Many new dads are so sensitive to criticism or nervous about getting it wrong that they quickly give up. But apart from breastfeeding, your partner can do all the baby chores as well as you can – if he's allowed to practise. If you find it hard to hand over your baby, especially if he starts to cry, or becomes fussy, leave the room – or even the house. Your partner needs the space and the time to build his confidence without you watching over his shoulder.

- **Try to be practical:** there's no point in you both being exhausted at the same time. Take it in turns during the week to get up for the baby, and try to organise it so that each of you has one lie-in at the weekend.

- **Split the responsibility over the weekend:** even if it's not possible to share daily events like drop-offs, bath time and bedtime because of the hours that you both work, make sure you share the jobs out at the weekend. Not only do you and your partner benefit from being involved in your child's life, you both get some free time, too – and your child benefits from getting the undivided attention of you both.

- **Keep each other in the loop:** when you are both busy, it's easy to forget to share vital information like your childcarer's holiday dates or the fact that chickenpox is going round the nursery. Anything that impacts on your life as a family needs to be shared, not only so you both feel involved, but also so you can both take on your share of the load if there are practical or emotional consequences.

> *'It's hard leaving Phoebe with Martin – she always cries, which upsets him, too. But I know if I do it regularly she'll get used to being without me.'*
>
> Sandra, financial consultant and
> mum to Phoebe, six months

Running the house

With both of you helping out, the amount of work is halved.

- **Think ahead:** before you go back to work, talk together about your expectations. If you've always done the housework before, discuss how hard it will be for you to continue managing alone.

- **Point out that you both have the same goal:** a relaxed and stress-free home environment – and that splitting the domestic workload is not only the most efficient way for the house to run smoothly, but also a way of helping you to be supportive and caring.

- **Be willing to compromise and negotiate:** this might mean lowering your standards, for example, and not always making the decisions.

- **Be patient and appreciative:** remember that change sometimes takes a while to get established.

Making time for each other

Your relationship can't thrive if you spend all your free time being 'mummy' or 'daddy'. This doesn't mean you have to leave the children for a week's holiday in Italy (much as you might love to!). Just taking time to be together – without a baby in your arms or a child tugging at your sleeve – is important. Spending uninterrupted time together is good for your relationship, which means it's good for your family, too.

- **Make time for intimacy:** with the physical demands of a baby or small child, you may feel you don't need so much physical contact with your partner, but, without physical intimacy, couples very often drift apart emotionally.

- **Spend time together:** try to spend some regular time together out of the house, without your baby. You could timetable a regular babysitter (or join a babysitting circle) so that you can go out together on a regular basis, even if it's just for an hour or so. Once it's booked into the diary you are less likely to cancel.

- **Switch off the TV:** in the evening, switching off the TV and having a takeaway together will give you the chance to chat without being distracted.

- **Ask grandparents to help out:** perhaps they could even care for your baby while you have a night away together. You may find it hard not to worry, but there's no reason to go far from home; the aim is simply to have an uninterrupted night in one another's company.

- **Treat yourselves:** get someone in to help with the ironing and/or cleaning. Then there's no excuse for not having time to enjoy each other's company.

- **Show you care:** let your partner know how much you love and appreciate him. Give him the occasional gift, make a loving phone call to his office, even run his bath! Being generous with your love and time will encourage him to be generous with his in return.

> '*Simon and I have had very little alone-time since Katie was born. But now I'm back at work we try to meet up for lunch once a week. I don't feel guilty because I'm not using up time I could spend with Katie, so I can really focus on Simon – and it feels quite romantic!*'
>
> Andrea, housing officer and mum to Katie, 15 months

Talking and listening

Spending time together is pretty pointless if you are not getting on. So what's the key to a healthy, happy relationship? Good communication certainly comes high on the list – and this doesn't just mean 'Don't forget to pick up more nappies from the shop, darling!' It's more about talking and listening – and staying in touch with your partner's feelings and thoughts.

- **Share your feelings:** don't assume he knows that, for example, you feel sad missing out on aspects of your child's life, or that you worry about money. Tell him you are not necessarily looking for answers, just a chance to share your feelings. Listen when he shares his concerns. You don't always need to solve the problem – just talking can help.

- **Be up front:** you can't read each other's minds, so if you need some help from him, you need to ask for it.

- **Sort out disagreements:** and do so sooner rather than later. Letting dissatisfaction stew can turn a small quarrel into a major clash.

- **Keep arguments productive:** while differences of opinion are natural, learning to compromise is a learnt skill. Avoid being personal (use 'I felt upset', rather than 'You made me upset'), don't use absolutes ('You never ... I always ...') and stick to the issue in hand.

- **Talk together about your hopes and dreams:** not just for the future, but for your next family holiday, weekend outing or family celebration.

Stay-at-home dads

If you are the main breadwinner in your relationship, and both you and your partner are keen to avoid full-time childcare, you may decide that the most practical solution is for him to stay at home and care for your child. In fact, there are an increasing number of stay-at-home dads – and many more, according to the latest research, who'd relish the opportunity to look after their children.

Although the loss of income may be an issue, there are huge benefits, too: you can relax at work knowing your child is getting the best possible care; you both have a shared goal, so are more willing to make sacrifices and changes to your lifestyle; you communicate better – he needs to tell you what's been happening all day, and you need to know; and your child gets to see that it's not just mummies who can cook and clean! You still, however, need to take care with your relationship.

- **Be patient and flexible:** with both of you taking on non-traditional gender roles, it's inevitable that you'll have to go through a period of adjustment. Finding ways to make it work will take time.

- **Be prepared to let go:** from caring for your child to the household chores, chances are your partner will do things differently to you but that doesn't mean what he's doing is wrong.

- **Be supportive and appreciative:** he has to feel confident about his role, and knowing that you think he's doing a great job will be a real boost for his self-esteem.

- **Be understanding:** bear in mind that life for a stay-at-home dad can be isolating. Take a day off now and again and go to the mother and baby/toddler group with him. Other mums may be more comfortable becoming his friend once they know you.

> *'Joe and I definitely have different priorities. I know if I were at home with Lucy, the house would be much cleaner and tidier. But having him caring for her is the only way I can happily work full time – and learning to live in a slightly messy house is worth the sacrifice.'*
>
> Cathy, dentist and mum to Lucy, two and a half

Being a single parent

Whether you've chosen to become a single parent, or have had single parenthood thrust upon you, yours is still a family like any other. And although coping alone – especially when you are working, too – can be very hard, and at times frightening, there can be positive aspects of being a single parent.

In the early days, for example, you will have only yourself to worry about. It'll be hard work, but also an incredibly special time as you and your baby settle and adapt into each other's rhythms. You will develop a very close relationship with your child, often doing more with her than two parents manage. You won't be torn between keeping your baby and partner happy. And while you may often wonder how life might have been different for your child with two parents, you can also remind yourself that children are happier if you are happy: no parent would wish their child to be stuck in the middle of a relationship going wrong.

The biggest problem for children of single parents is often low income, which is why having a job can make all the difference. But even without financial worries, bringing up children on your own can be exhausting and lonely. Planning ahead for difficult times and trying to stay in control of your life will help to make it work.

● **Build up a good support network:** make a list of everyone you know, and how they can help. Include parents, siblings, old friends, new friends, neighbours, health visitors and community services. Imagine who you would contact when you need help – whether it's practical advice, a shoulder to cry on, a lift to the shops or company on holiday. Just knowing someone's available for you will help ease anxiety and loneliness.

- **Take good care of yourself:** your baby is relying on you, and the healthier and happier you are, the more love and attention you will be able to give him. Routines are important. Have healthy meals at regular times, take regular exercise and get plenty of rest.

- **Get involved in your child's life:** use days off work to do this. Your antenatal group, church or local mother and toddler group are good places to meet people and make friends. As your child gets older, the school's Parent Teacher Association (PTA) often needs extra helpers and is a great way to build friendships.

- **Have time away from your baby:** work doesn't count. You still need a social life – although having one may take some organisation. Joining a babysitting circle will help keep costs down and going out with friends, going to see a film and having some 'me time' will be incredibly refreshing as well as giving you the space to put any worries or problems into perspective.

'Ben is the most important person in my life, and I've never regretted being a single mum, even though it's hard work. But I am lucky – my parents are very much there for me. Without them, going back to work would have been impossible. Now, money is one thing I don't need to worry about.'

Zoe, intensive care nurse and mum to Ben, four

SUMMARY OF CHAPTER 9

- The first year after birth can be the rockiest time for many relationships.
- Sharing the load – parenting and chores – can help prevent resentment.
- Spend time together to help keep your relationship strong and happy.
- If your partner is a stay-at-home dad, you need to appreciate the unique challenges he has to face.
- If you are a single mum, you need to plan ahead and stay in control.

CHAPTER 10

The Early Years:
What You Need to Know

By now you may feel that you are in the swing of being a working mother. However, the rules of motherhood dictate that no sooner do you feel you are on top of things, than another challenge comes along.

Minor childhood illnesses like colds and tummy upsets can be especially challenging for working mums because they are unpredictable and force you to drop everything to take care of your ailing child. As she grows, you'll also need to think about pre-school and school nursery applications and deal with the disruption this will bring to your childcare arrangements.

One way to cope with the ups and downs of working and being a mother is to streamline your babycare routine. Aim to do all the basic things – food, sleep, playing with your child and enjoying her company – really well, rather than striving to be the best mum in the world. After all, no child was ever harmed by having a shop-bought birthday cake rather than a homemade one, or by going off to nursery in un-ironed clothes.

If the stress of it all starts to get to you, don't try to soldier on regardless. As a working mother some stress in your life is inevitable, but chronic stress is harmful for you, your relationship and your little one. Take it as a warning: you are doing too much and it's time to make some changes in your life.

Caring for your child

The renowned child development expert Donald Winnicott once said that babies don't need perfect mothers in order to grow up healthy and happy; they just need 'good-enough' mothers. It's a useful mantra for working mothers everywhere and one to bear in mind next time you are chastising yourself for giving your little one the same meal two days in a row or forgetting to brush her teeth.

As a working mum you may not have as much time with your baby or toddler as a stay-at-home mum, but provided your child has high-quality childcare while you are at work, there's no evidence to suggest she'll lose out in any way. What it does mean, though, is that you probably won't have time for luxuries like beautifully co-ordinated baby outfits each day or hand-prepared organic food at every meal.

The trick is to work out what basics your baby or toddler really needs and then aim to do these really well. It will also help if you build a good, solid routine for yourself and your baby, so that mealtimes, bedtime and so on all become second nature.

- Bath time needn't be daily unless it's an integral part of your little one's bedtime routine. Three times a week should be plenty. Drop everything, relax and enjoy playing and splashing with your child.

- The odd jar of baby food or slice of pizza won't hurt, but aim to give unprocessed foods as often as possible. Batch-cooking food at weekends and freezing it into portions is probably the easiest way to do this.

- Make sure she gets her sleep. If your other half arrives home at bedtime wanting to play rough and tumble with your little one, lay down the law and insist on quiet activities like reading and singing before bed.

- Make sure your child goes to bed at the same time each night, including at weekends.

- If your baby or toddler goes to a childminder or nursery, check her bag each night to make sure it contains everything needed for the next day.

- Make sure you take your child for all the developmental checks and vaccinations. It's easy to slip behind with the schedule when you are working, but make it a priority and they will all be over and done with quicker.

- Keep your house free of smoke. Young children are more likely to develop health problems, such as coughing and wheezing, if exposed to cigarette smoke.

- Make sure your baby or toddler gets some fresh air. Check with your carer that your child has trips out or at least a chance to play outside each day. As well as encouraging exercise, this will also make sure she gets the vitamin D she needs from sunlight.

- Breastfeed for as long as you can – breastfed babies tend to have fewer infections in childhood and enjoy better health as adults.

- When you do have time with your baby or toddler, forget about the educational toys and stimulating activities. Just get down on the floor with her, play with her, chat, laugh, cuddle and enjoy each other's company.

- If you work part time, arrange your days so that you can attend a baby or toddler group together – that way you'll both make new friends.

Coping with childhood illness

Nobody warns you before you become a mother just how prone babies and toddlers are to minor illnesses: it's said that babies can catch up to ten colds in their first year alone! No sooner does a tummy bug clear up than a sniffle or a cough comes along. Your child's immune system won't be sufficiently developed to fight off bacteria and viruses in a similar way as an adult's until she's about five or six.

Young children tend to become ill quite rapidly, so you often have little warning that they are sickening for something. Your baby may be fine when you put her to bed, only to wake with a raging temperature an hour later. They can also go downhill quite quickly when they are ill, so it's important to get things like fever, vomiting and diarrhoea checked out promptly by your GP. Add to this the fact that young children have a tendency to get ill just before important meetings and you have a potential nightmare on your hands.

The best way to deal with childhood illnesses is to accept that they are going to be part of your life for a while and plan ahead for them. Speak to your childcarer about whether or not she is prepared to have your child when she's ill. You'll probably find that carers who care for children in the home are more inclined to take poorly children than nurseries, which care for larger numbers of children. If your carer is not happy to have your child when she's poorly, you and your partner will need to be prepared for caring for your child yourself.

Talk about how you will manage this. Will you take it in turns to care for your child when she's ill? Or will you do one day on and one day off? Talk to your respective managers about whether you will be entitled to time off for dependants (see page 71) or whether you will need to take either parental or annual leave. Sick babies tend to sleep a lot, so another possibility is for one of you to work at home if your baby is taken poorly. Just in case, you may want to make sure that you have access to all your contact details and can access your e-mails at home.

> 'Whenever Arjun gets a cold, I always end up with one as well and life gets very difficult for a while. I love my work, but when your child is ill he has to come first.'
>
> Shivani, secondary school teacher and mum to Arjun, two

Juggling pre-school and childcare

If your baby is cared for in a nursery while you are at work, she'll have plenty of toys, activities and company of her own age to stimulate her. If she's cared for by a nanny or childminder, however, you may feel that she needs more stimulation and more opportunities to mix with other children than one person can offer.

Around the age of three, many parents consider enrolling their child into a part-time pre-school. Many nurseries and playgroups offer part-time sessions in the morning and afternoon. Morning sessions tend to be most popular, and therefore most oversubscribed, as many three-year-olds are still having naps in the afternoon.

Pre-schools have a slightly later start than schools, usually at around 9.30am, which means that you will still need your carer to drop your child off, or you will need to rearrange your working hours so that you can drop her off yourself. One of the main advantages of doing the drop-off yourself is that you will get to meet other parents. Lots of children start to form their first friendships around the age of three, and this is a good opportunity to invite your child's friend round to play. It will also help to keep you plugged in to the pre-school grapevine in your area: if there's chickenpox going round, or someone's had a new baby or there's a new toddler music group in the area, nursery or playgroup drop-off time is the best time to find out.

> '*Nick and I have rearranged our hours so that I drop Louis off at the nursery, the childminder picks him up, then Nick picks him up from the childminder's at 5pm. It's great, because we both get a bit of quality time with him each day.*'
>
> Malgosia, knitwear designer and mum to Louis, three

Many established childminders have good relationships with their local pre-schools and are very happy to take children to and from sessions. In some ways it's a useful trial run for when your child starts 'big school'. If you use a nanny, though, she may be unhappy about taking a drop in salary to look after your child for only part of the day. You have several options here:

- Continue to pay her the same as before.

- Agree a cut in pay on the understanding that she will seek other work elsewhere (that hopefully complements your child's hours).

- Speak to friends to see if you can set up a nanny share.
- Have another baby!

Managing stress

Once you become a working mum, stress becomes a fact of life. It's common to feel that you simply have too much to fit into your days. Or you may feel that you are failing in one or more of the various roles in you life: wife, mother, employee, daughter, member of playgroup committee, pet carer. Stress can come out of the blue – when your childcarer calls to say she's ill, for example – or it can be the result of long-term pressures, such as a heavy workload or a poor relationship with your manager.

Provided it's not long term and chronic, stress can actually be a good thing. The adrenalin surge it brings helps to cut through tiredness and spurs you to get things done. It can also be a useful signal that something needs changing in your life. If your long commute causes your blood pressure to rise each morning, for instance, it's time to look for work nearer home.

However, too much stress can have an adverse effect your health, relationships and lifestyle. It's not good for your baby or toddler to have a stressed-out mum, either. You may notice that you are:

- having more headaches than usual
- having difficulty sleeping
- rapidly losing or gaining weight
- jumpy, and that your heart sometimes races or your hands shake
- constantly feeling overstretched and tired
- having digestive problems, such as indigestion
- unable to concentrate
- snappy and irritable.

If stress is becoming an ongoing problem for you, it's important to do something about it. Even small changes in your lifestyle can make a huge difference.

● **Identify the cause:** see if you can work out what's causing you to feel stressed and think about how you could eliminate these things from your life.

● **Develop five-minute strategies:** for when you feel you are about to snap. These could be sitting quietly and breathing deeply for a few minutes, walking round the block or locking the bathroom door and taking a long bath.

● **Talk:** don't keep it all to yourself. Talk to your partner, friends or relatives about how you are feeling – they may have useful support and advice to offer you.

● **Try to eat healthily:** getting the nutrients you need will help you to stay sound of mind as well as body.

● **Avoid smoking and drinking:** these habits may reduce your stress in the short term, but in the end they will do more harm than good.

● **Get some exercise:** one of the best de-stressors there is. It helps to raise your mood and flush stress-related hormones out of your system. It also helps to relax your muscles and promote good sleep.

● **Plan a treat:** make sure you always have a treat in your diary – book a spa day with a friend, take half a day off work to go shopping or book your holiday early. Whenever you feel stressed, spend a few lovely moments thinking about the treat you've got in store.

● **Try not to be too hard on yourself:** the more perfectionist you are about your home, work and mothering skills, the more stressed you are likely to feel. Cut yourself some slack and let your standards drop for a while.

'Whenever Martin goes out, I get out my Lost *DVDs and turn our living room into a spa. I sit there and paint my nails or massage my feet and all my worries melt away for a while.'*

Jennie, shop manager and mum to Joseph, seven, William, three, and Laura, eight months

SUMMARY OF CHAPTER 10

- Aim to be a 'good-enough' mother rather than a perfect one and keep your babycare routine pared down and simple.
- Little children get lots of minor illnesses, and they're easier to cope with if you work out a strategy in advance.
- Putting your child into a playgroup may mean you need to rearrange your routine and childcare arrangements.
- Some stress can be motivational, but too much is bad for you and needs to be addressed.

CHAPTER 11

Everyday Family Life: The Nuts and Bolts

There's no getting away from it: when you are a working mum, trying to get everything done – when you want, how you want – is like trying to squeeze toothpaste back into its tube. It is virtually impossible and trying to do it can send you mad. Instead, making everyday family life work is about accepting that it'll never be perfect, but it can be good. The key is to get organised, accept compromise (especially when it comes to housework and meals), stop work from intruding on family time, and give yourself a break, whenever you can.

Getting organised

Having enough time to keep your home and work life running smoothly depends on being well organised. This doesn't mean running your house like a military operation – being free to be spontaneous when the mood takes you is what makes life fun. But the better organised you are, the more free time you have – and the less chance there is of forgetting to do those things (whether it's remembering to pay the milkman, returning that phone call, or buying your mum's birthday present) that help keep life trouble free.

- **Give the house a good clear-out:** do this before you go back to work. The less clutter there is around, the easier it is to find a place for everything – and you'll have more chance of remembering where everything is.

- **Organise your home filing:** it doesn't need to be neat or involve a recognisable system; it just has to be logical for you. The acid test is whether or not you could explain over the phone where you've put something.

- **Pay bills by direct debit:** this will save you time, and prevent you forgetting to pay a bill!

- **Make lists:** whether you use an electronic or personal organiser, or a large notebook, writing down what needs doing, from signing your child up for a music class to giving some thought to your summer holiday, means you don't have to think about it again until you have time to look at your list and get it done.

- **List phone numbers:** if you need to make phone calls, list the numbers, too. And take the list everywhere with you – you never know when you might have a free moment (waiting in the car to pick up from ballet/football/school) to make one of those calls.

- **Prioritise important tasks:** try to get these out of the way as quickly as possible so that you no longer have to worry about them.

- **Don't do anything rash:** even the most organised person occasionally feels overwhelmed by all the demands of family life and work. If this happens, don't do anything foolish, like handing in your notice at work. Instead take some time out on you own – have a quiet lunch or take a walk – to get it all into perspective.

'I have an A4 hardback notebook with my work to-do list at the front and my home to-do list at the back. I take it everywhere with me – and try to tick at least one thing off every day.'

Liz, chief executive of a primary care trust and mum to Jack, 15, and Miranda, 14

Keeping on top of chores

Ideally, you'd like to come home from work to a tidy, clean and welcoming house, and sit down to enjoy a delicious home-cooked meal with your family. Inevitably, however, there are times when there is no food in the fridge, the table is buried under clutter and you feel like sitting down and crying. Running a house can be tiring, and relentless – and sometimes it only takes a few moments with your eyes off the ball for the whole place to sink into utter chaos. So how do you stay on top of everyday chores, and avoid them sapping both your energy and your morale? (Please note – all of these tips apply equally to loving, supportive partners!)

Housework

- **Only worry about the absolute minimum:** everyone can live with a few cobwebs, but no one wants to have to put dirty underwear back on in the morning.

- **Have a routine:** and stick to it. For example, emptying the laundry basket every morning on your way downstairs or allocating half an hour a day for one chore (dusting, vacuuming, cleaning toilets).

- **Develop good habits:** every time you go upstairs take something with you (children's toys, a batch of ironed clothes, toiletries from the supermarket) and bring something down (an armful of washing, dirty cups, a bin that needs emptying).

- **Keep a duster handy:** have one upstairs as well as down. If the urge takes you, you can then fish it out of the drawer and do a bit of cleaning while waiting for the bath to run.

- **Decide what's important to you:** and concentrate on that. If clutter gets you down, ignore the cobwebs but clear the carpet of toys before you collapse on the sofa.

- **Factor in a treat:** this can help if you are feeling grumpy about the housework. Promise yourself a glass of wine once you've cleaned the bathroom, listen to music while you do the ironing, keep a pot of expensive hand cream on the windowsill to use after you've washed up.

- **Get your children involved:** as soon as they can physically manage, insist your children make their own bed every morning, put dirty clothes in the laundry basket, hang their towel up, help lay the table, put their dirty dishes on the side and tuck their chair in when they get down from the table. Bear in mind, however, that you need to be persistent – it'll take gentle reminders every day for at least a few weeks before these things become a habit.

- **Get rid of shoddy equipment:** a decent vacuum cleaner, floor mop and iron can make tasks quicker and easier.

- **Have regular clear-outs:** the less stuff you have in the house, the less there is that needs tidying.

- **Employ someone:** if it all gets too much, get in a cleaner, gardener or someone to do the ironing. If your finances don't stretch to regular help, go for a once-a-month blitz from the professionals.

- **Remember that you don't have to be superwoman:** (or superman). Your house isn't a show home, so just do what's important to you, concentrate on getting that done, and enjoy your home.

Mealtimes

- **Plan meals in advance:** if you know what you are cooking each evening, you can keep on top of the shopping, and even get in some preparation the night before or first thing in the morning.

- **Look out for quick and easy recipes:** there are plenty of food magazines and recipe websites offering ideas for fast, healthy meals.

- **Use an internet delivery service:** for a few extra pounds, getting your food delivered to the door can save you a couple of hours a week.

- **Take short cuts where you can:** jars of sauce, frozen pastry and ready-prepared vegetables, for example, can help you save time without compromising the food.

- **Make use of your freezer:** when you do have time to cook from scratch, double the quantities (sponge cake, pastry, bolognaise sauce) and stick half in the freezer ready for another day.

- **Get your children to help:** turn cooking at the weekend into a family affair. Let your children help choose a recipe, and then they can help you to get it ready.

> 'I have a bread maker – which sounds mad, but I set the timer so that when I walk through the front door after work the house is full of the aroma of freshly made bread. This makes me feel so much better about serving up fish fingers for tea – again!'
>
> Kitty, book publisher and mum
> to Olivia, 12, and Fanny, three

Keeping work and home separate

Whether or not you can forget about work at the front door will depend to a certain extent on how much responsibility you have. Rightly or wrongly, the further up the career ladder you climb, the more tends to be expected of you in terms of hours – out-of-hours meetings, calls at home, and being made to feel like a truant when you leave the office on time. But your children need to know that when you are at home, they – and not your boss – are the most important people in your life. So how do you keep work and home life separate?

- **Be very clear about your boundaries:** once you invite colleagues or your boss to contact you at home, it will be harder to refuse in the future.

- **Be assertive:** if early morning or late afternoon meetings are hard for you, be firm and tell your colleagues – only those who are unreasonable will find this difficult to accept.

- **Keep your answer machine on:** you can then return calls when it's convenient for you. A system that tells you who the caller is can help you screen calls, too.

- **Have a separate phone line for your business:** if you work from home.

- **Plan for holidays:** get organised at work before holidays to avoid problems arising while you are away.

- **Take your holidays abroad:** if you are in a position to choose! This will make you less easy to contact, and there will be less temptation to get back to the office and sort the problem out.

- **Switch the computer off:** avoid having your computer on at home when the children are around – once it's humming away, the temptation to check e-mails will be hard to resist.

- **Switch off your mobile:** when you walk through the front door, switch off your phone and/or BlackBerry.

- **Deal with problems:** if you find switching off difficult and are suffering from work-related stress, try to deal with the problems as soon as possible before they start impacting on your family life, too.

> *'I always leave the office on time – but I regularly have to bring work home. I am strict with myself, though, I don't go to my computer until the children are in bed and, if I need to catch up with work at the weekend, I get up earlier and deal with it before the children wake up.'*
>
> Nicola, probation officer and
> mum to Jonty, four, and Anna, ten

Finding time for yourself

All too easily, work and caring for your children can absorb your every waking minute. Parents' evening is suddenly the main social event in your calendar, supper is the children's leftovers and picking up and dropping off at various after-school activities the only exercise you get. Soon all your reserves – not just of energy but enthusiasm for family life – are exhausted. Making time for yourself – whether it's to enjoy a decent meal, or have a night out with friends – is vital, but never easy. Here are some suggestions on how to make it work (see also page 83).

- **Don't feel guilty:** everyone, including your children, partner and boss, benefit when you make time for yourself.

- **Eat properly:** if you don't want to cook two meals (one for the children, one for you and your partner), either give the children a snack when they are back from school to keep them going and have supper later as a family, or find suppers that everyone enjoys so you can reheat yours later.

- **Take exercise:** you know that exercise is not only good for your health but can also make you feel more energetic, so get creative with your time and get fit. Double up on family activities: for example, take the children swimming (if they are very little, team up with a friend) and do ten laps by yourself; have a regular bouncing session on their trampoline (a great aerobic work-out); take the children to the park, and while they play, run ten times round the perimeter; take them on a cycle ride but leave your bike at home and run alongside them instead.

- **Plan ahead:** making commitments (booking a Pilates course, agreeing to host a book club) makes it harder to cancel and less likely that you'll sacrifice your own plans to accommodate your children or partner.

- **Swap time with your partner:** you could each have a 'me' weekend once a month when only one of you has to be available for children and chores. Even if you just spend the time pottering in the garden or clearing out your wardrobe, being able to focus on something you get pleasure doing without interruption or distraction can be very relaxing. If you are a single mum, do the same with a friend who has children of a similar age.

- **Rethink your work/life balance:** if work impinges so much on your home life that all this seems impossible, you need to rethink your work/life balance. Perhaps it's time to try to renegotiate your hours (see Chapter 6).

SUMMARY OF CHAPTER 11

- Getting – and keeping – your house organised will give you more free time and help keep life running smoothly.
- Having a routine, getting your children to help, and accepting you can't be superwoman helps you to stay on top of the chores.
- Eat healthily without too much work by planning ahead, internet shopping and using short cuts whenever possible.
- Keeping work and home separate reminds your family that they – and not your boss – are the most important people in your life.
- Finding time for yourself is good for you and good for your family.

CHAPTER 12

Behaviour: Getting the Best from Your Child

When you've had a difficult day at work, an unco-operative child can push you to the limit. You end up either giving into her demands or losing your rag. Neither outcome makes you feel good about yourself.

There are of course certain times of the day when everyone's stress level rises. The morning rush is one. Getting back home after school and work is another. Giving your children a snack often helps improve their mood. A cup of tea, a sit down and a chat will probably help yours. But then there's teatime, bath time and bedtime still to contend with – lots of opportunities for your child to dig her heels in and be difficult.

Handling your child's behaviour – especially at moments like these – is an art that takes time and practice to perfect. So even if you've read all the parenting books and watched all the parenting programmes around, there will be times when those brilliant strategies for getting your child to do what you want fly out of your head and you stand there ranting at her instead.

When this happens, remind yourself that becoming a great parent is a learning curve, and a steep one, too. Forgive yourself. Then take some time to think about how you could have handled the situation differently – so next time your parenting skills are put to the test, you are a bit more prepared.

Managing everyday behaviour

Here are some simple strategies to help you encourage your child to behave well.

- **Use praise:** find opportunities to praise your child for good behaviour, and do it immediately. Young children especially learn this way. If, for example, your child asks nicely for the jam at the breakfast table, you could say 'Well done for remembering to say please and thank you.'

- **Use rewards and privileges:** use these to show your appreciation. Perhaps if your 12-year-old offers to run to the shop to pick up a pint of milk, you could let her have some extra time on the computer.

- **Ignore minor misdemeanours:** whenever you can, let these pass without comment. Children can sometimes be irritating just to get your attention, and constantly nagging or disciplining not only helps them achieve their aim but also creates a negative mood. Instead pretend you haven't noticed.

- **Distract or redirect your child:** the behaviour of young children especially can be managed in this way. If, for example, you know your youngest always wants whichever toy her older sister has chosen to play with, be ready with something equally interesting to grab her attention.

> *'My mum pointed out how negative I was with Will. He can be quite cheeky and disobedient, and I used to imagine the dreadful trouble he'd get into when he was older if he carried on behaving like that. I now try harder to look for the good things he does and make sure he knows when I'm pleased. He's still no angel, but he is better.'*
>
> Tricia, indexer and mum to Will, eight

Setting clear limits and boundaries

Your child can only behave well when she's clear what's expected of her, and this means you need to make sure she knows what is and isn't allowed and exactly what the limits are.

Some boundaries you choose to set will be age specific. Young children, for example, need boundaries to keep them safe ('You can't cross the road unless I'm holding your hand'). Older children need limits to help them learn to be fair ('Everyone deserves a piece of cake, so it must be shared equally), considerate ('You need to ring me when you arrive at your friend's house so I know you are safe') and responsible ('Having your own room is a privilege, and I expect you to keep it tidy yourself').

The following should make it easier for your child to stick within the limits.

- **Establish routines:** expect to spend a few days reminding your child (just saying it once or twice may not be enough) to make her bed first thing in the morning, hang her coat up when she comes in or do her homework before she watches the television. These habits will then become ingrained.

- **Be consistent:** once you've established a rule (bed at nine, piano practice before play, asking before using the phone), stick with it. There will be plenty of occasions when your child begs for flexibility and occasionally there may be very good reasons for being flexible. But bear in mind that if you give in once without good reason, it will become increasingly difficult to stick to your guns in the future.

- **Review the rules as your child grows up:** what's right for a toddler isn't necessarily right for a seven-year-old. And as children develop more independence, it's important that they are given as much freedom as possible within reasonable limits.

- **Involve your child in decision-making:** although you should always have the final say, your child needs to know that opinions count. And being given the chance to question, discuss and ask for reasons and explanations will help your child to accept the final decision.

> '*I have very firm rules about tidiness. I don't have enough time to run around tidying up after my children. If they leave something lying around, I put it on the bottom of the stairs and if it hasn't been put away after a day it goes in the bin!*'
>
> Christina, IT specialist and mum to Sammy, 14, and Flossie, nine

Reacting fairly

All children get it wrong sometimes. Younger ones often simply forget that, for example, they've been asked not to run inside the house with muddy shoes, to flush the loo after using it or to eat with a knife and fork, not their fingers.

Older children want to feel as if they, not you, are in control of their lives, and try to assert themselves by lounging in front of the television instead of getting on with their homework and spending their lunch money on crisps and chocolate rather than a hot meal.

Often you can find yourself taking on the role of the metaphorical punch ball. Your child has had an argument with a friend, is overtired and grumpy, feels you haven't been paying her much attention recently or has had a bad day at school. Taking her frustration out on you is a safe bet – she knows you won't hold it against her. But, at the same time, this can be difficult for you to cope with.

Whatever the offence, it's important to react fairly. After all, the purpose of disciplining children is to help them see the consequences of their actions, and encourage them to behave better the next time.

● **Stay calm:** try to be calm and kind but firm. Your child will understand your point of view better if she can focus on what you are saying rather than how you are saying it. Although it's natural to feel angry when your child has behaved badly, speaking harshly will upset her, and make her defensive.

- **Think before you speak:** a rush of anger can result in a bad choice of words or an inappropriate punishment. If your emotions are running so high you can't act calmly, ask your child to go to her room until you feel ready to talk to her about the issue.

- **Apologise:** if you do blow a fuse, and it is inevitable there will be times when this happens, apologise as quickly as you can. Don't blame your child for your anger. Seeing you take responsibility for your emotions will help her learn how to control hers.

- **Be realistic:** all children make mistakes, and small mistakes may only need to be pointed out.

- **Use appropriate discipline:** if you feel discipline of some form is necessary (see page 117), make sure that it's appropriate for your child's age, personality and the seriousness of the offence.

- **Don't hold grudges:** avoid making your child feel guilty. If you explain clearly and firmly to your child why you are upset, she is more likely to understand your point of view. Holding a grudge will simply leave her feeling hopeless, resentful and less motivated to change her behaviour.

> *'Occasionally, especially when I'm tired, I get very snappy with the girls. But I always apologise afterwards. Now, if one of them gets in a fury and yells at me, they usually say sorry afterwards, which I really appreciate.'*
>
> Cate, optician and mum to Stephanie and Emily, both 12

Resolving disagreements

Families bicker and argue – it's a fact of life. Only the issues will vary, depending on your child's age, stage and personality. Sometimes the disagreements will be minor – your child wants a biscuit but tea is nearly ready so the answer is no. She knows the family rules are no snacking between meals, so that should be the end of the argument. Sometimes, however, disagreements will arise over issues you may not yet have had a chance to tackle. For example, your child doesn't feel like going to her piano lesson tonight, or your teenager has planned a sleepover without checking with you first.

Learning to resolve disagreements effectively with minimum tears and tantrums (from you and your child!) is important not only for maintaining your relationship with your child but also for teaching her valuable skills that she will be able to use throughout her life.

- **Find a solution:** remember that coming up with an answer that you can both live with is more important than winning the battle. Trying to prove that you are right and your child is wrong can blow an argument out of all proportion.

- **Identify the problem:** it can be all too easy to over-react and blow up over side issues that have nothing to do with the central disagreement. Let your child explain freely what the problem is – 'I don't want to go to my piano lesson because I didn't practise this week' or 'I've already invited my friends over for the sleepover. It'll be so embarrassing telling them they can't come.'

- **Voice your child's feelings:** 'You are upset because …', 'You feel that …' – so that your child knows you understand her point of view.

- **Explain your point of view:** 'Even if you haven't done any practice it's still worth going', 'Checking with me beforehand about sleepovers gives me the chance to make arrangements so your fun doesn't impinge on the rest of the family.'

- **Work together to solve the problem:** brainstorm ideas that would be acceptable to you both, even though you both may have to compromise. For example, perhaps your child could say to her piano teacher that she's been very busy this week and hasn't been able to do as much practice as normal, and maybe your teenager could have a sleepover next week rather than this week.

Enforcing discipline

However hard you try to be positive and encourage good behaviour, to respond fairly when she makes mistakes and to resolve disagreements, there will be occasions when you need to act to make it clear that what your child did is unacceptable and won't be tolerated.

A generation or so ago, smacking was seen as an acceptable way of disciplining a child. Nowadays most parents accept that smacking does nothing to help children learn how to improve their behaviour. In fact, all it does is confuse a child who has been taught that physical violence (biting her sister, hitting a friend) is unacceptable.

Today's less punitive attitude to discipline does, however, have its own problems. No parent wants to damage their relationship with their child, and for some this can make saying 'no' difficult. But when it comes to showing your child that her actions have consequences, being a great mum means being prepared to be unpopular at times.

Stay calm

Unless you've had the chance to calm down and think about the situation rationally and objectively, it's impossible to discipline your child fairly, in a way that will allow your child to learn from the experience.

Tell your child what she has done wrong

Although your child may often be quite clear about her misbehaviour, there may be times when she is genuinely confused about why she is in trouble. Explain why her behaviour is not acceptable. This may be because it was dangerous, hurtful, rude or provocative. If your child is capable, ask her to think about and explain the consequences of her actions.

Decide on an appropriate level of discipline

This should be done calmly and rationally, and should be judged on the severity of the 'offence', whether or not it was committed without thinking, or whether it has been committed repeatedly and deliberately. Here are some suggestions.

- **A verbal warning:** ask your child not to repeat the behaviour and remind her that if she does, the punishment will be more severe. This gives your child the chance to behave properly.

- **Making amends:** if your child has upset someone, she needs to find a way of making that person feel better. If she ran across the floor with muddy feet, she can wipe up the mess. This can, for example, prove the point that it's often less hassle to avoid misbehaving in the first place.

- **Time out:** send your child out of the room for a period of time. This can give your child the chance to calm down and think about what she has done. This may be more suitable for a younger child.

- **Banning treats or privileges:** take away something your child loves (sweets, television, computer, pocket money, going out with friends, having friends round) for a couple of days, a week or longer. It can also help to ask your child a few questions at the end of the ban period like, 'Do you remember why your behaviour was inappropriate?' or 'Can I trust you not to misbehave in this way again?'.

'I really hate punishing the children, but I realise that setting limits now will make life easier for all of us as they get older.'

Peggy, design engineer and mum to Zara, nine, and Jacob, six

SUMMARY OF CHAPTER 12

- Use praise and rewards to encourage good behaviour, and be prepared to ignore the odd misdemeanour.
- Set clear boundaries so that your child knows what is expected of her.
- React fairly to bad behaviour and try to remain calm.
- Learn to resolve disagreements by working together.
- When discipline is necessary, ensure that it is appropriate.

CHAPTER 13

Work: Be a Great Mum *and* Succeed

B ecoming a mum tends to give you a different perspective on work. Yes, it may still be very important to you, but now you have an even more important job to do at home – caring for your child. This can cause tensions with non-parent colleagues who may be irritated by your rapid exits at the end of each day and sudden disappearances when your child's carer or school calls to say he is ill.

You may also find that your manager expects you to work in exactly the same way as you did before you became a mother – doing long hours, socialising in the evenings, travelling long distances for meetings, taking work home at weekends and so on. If these things are an accepted part of the culture in your workplace it can be hard to go against the tide. Do remember, though, that with all the new skills you have learned as a parent and as an experienced member of staff, you are of great value to your employer and it is not in their interests to disregard your needs. After all, you will work far more productively if you feel valued and supported.

Your working day

As a working mum you seem constantly to be dashing from one place to another: from home to nursery, from nursery to work, from work to the supermarket, back to the nursery and finally home again. One way to avoid feeling like a headless chicken is to build some slack into your day. Set your alarm half an hour earlier than usual to give yourself a good head start, arrange to leave your child a little earlier with her carer, then catch a bus or train that gives you plenty of time to get into work on time. Even better, get in a little early: sitting at your desk as your colleagues arrive will give you a huge psychological advantage when you head for the door at 5pm.

Lots of people hate commuting, but for us working mums it's a useful buffer zone that allows us to switch between 'mummy' and 'work' modes. It's also a great opportunity for a little downtime. For a few precious minutes you can spend your time as you please, listening to music, reading or even just thinking. Or you could use the time more constructively, perhaps to study or to pursue a new interest.

Similarly, when you are used to a little person demanding your attention every five minutes, a whole luxurious hour to yourself at lunchtime can seem too good to be true. Don't waste it by sitting at your desk with a sandwich or traipsing round the supermarket. Instead, enjoy a lunch out with friends or colleagues, do a little window-shopping or perhaps sign yourself up for an exercise class.

In some workplaces, there seem to be more important decisions taken and promotions decided in the pub after work than during the working day. When you are leaving at 5pm on the dot each day it's easy to start feeling excluded. If you feel a little left out, try some of the following.

- **Use lunchtime:** suggest going for lunch occasionally rather than having trips out after work.

- **Surprise your colleagues:** bring some sticky buns into work, make a cup of tea for everyone and hold an impromptu tea party.

- **Plan ahead:** make sure that you get big social events, such as Christmas parties, into your diary well in advance so that you can organise childcare and join in the fun.

- **Have the odd night out:** ask your partner to pick your child up from her carer now and again so that you can go along to some of the evening socials.

- **Keep up with the gossip:** when you do miss out on a work social, make sure you catch up on all the gossip next time you are in.

> *'My friends at work know I can't get out in the evenings now, so we've started going for a pizza on Friday lunchtimes. I love it. We have a laugh and it really lifts my week.'*
>
> Charmaine, office manager and mum to Jamal, eight, and Romane, one

Managing your time

Working mums are used to juggling priorities, and making sure you manage your time well at work will help to keep your stress levels down.

- **Make a daily to-do list:** it's a cliché, but too few of us do it. Only include really pressing tasks and leave out anything that can wait until another day. Keep a list of less urgent tasks elsewhere and, as they increase in urgency, transfer them to your daily to-do list.

- **Divide up tasks:** if there's a task on your to-do list that is so daunting you keep putting it off, break it down into smaller components and put these on your list, instead.

- **Concentrate on important tasks:** for really urgent tasks, block out a chunk of time in your diary, put your phone on answerphone and ask not to be disturbed for a while.

- **Limit e-mail time:** if you find you are constantly distracted by e-mails, keep your e-mail application shut and only open it to check e-mails at specific times of the day.

- **Take breaks:** schedule tea breaks and a proper lunch hour into your day. Regular breaks will help you stay productive.

- **Delegate:** where possible, ask other people to do things for you. People often feel they can do things quicker and better themselves, but these are the same people who complain of having too much on their plates!

- **Focus:** concentrate on one task at a time and aim to finish each task before you start on the next.

- **Talk to your manager:** if you feel you are managing your time efficiently, but still can't cope with your workload, make an appointment to discuss it with your manager. You may want to jot down which aspects of the work are unmanageable, plus a few possible solutions before the meeting.

Talking to your manager

Both you and your manager will find it helpful if you explain your home situation clearly from the start. If your manager doesn't have children, he or she may not realise, for example, that you will be fined if you pick your child up late from nursery. You may also want to forewarn your manager that young children are particularly prone to infectious illnesses and that you may need to take leave or work from home to cover this from time to time.

If other issues come up – if, for example, your partner is going to be away for a while and you will need to get into work later than usual – don't just knobble your manager as he or she walks past your desk. Instead, arrange a brief meeting so that you can explain your position clearly and in full. This will show that you take your needs as a parent seriously and, hopefully, encourage your manager to do the same.

Meetings, meetings, meetings

Most people hate meetings, but when you are only working part time or a meeting is dragging on at the end of the day, they can be particularly trying. Consider these strategies when constant meetings are threatening your sanity.

- **Be direct:** if a meeting clashes with your responsibilities as a mum, there's no need to blush and start muttering excuses about MMR jabs or school plays. Simply say you are busy at that time and suggest some alternative times that would suit you better.

- **Try teleconferencing:** if meetings constantly take you out of town, suggest teleconferencing instead, and offer to investigate how this can best be done.

- **Leave when you have to:** when attending a meeting in the late afternoon, forewarn the person leading the meeting that you need to leave at a certain time, then simply stand up and leave quietly when that time comes.

- **Offer to chair:** if you find that meetings tend to drag on, offer to chair some yourself or suggest you join meetings just for the part that is relevant to you.

Learn to be assertive

Assertiveness is all about getting your own needs met without trampling on other people's. It's about taking responsibility for yourself and your actions, and expressing yourself honestly and clearly without being afraid of the consequences. The only way to become more assertive is to practise. Next time you feel worried about doing or saying something, bite the bullet and do it anyway. You may be pleasantly surprised by the results.

Brush up your communication skills

Being able to communicate well at work is a great skill for anyone to have, and it's especially helpful when you are having to juggle the demands of work and home. Getting what you want to say across in a clear, direct and pleasant way will not only keep your relationships with your non-parent colleagues sweet, it will also make sure that you get your needs as a working parent met.

Start saying no

Does the word 'yes' seems to pop out of your mouth whenever someone asks you to do something? Saying yes all the time only means that you end up taking on too much and then feel angry or martyred. Get used to saying no when you already have a lot on your plate. It will help if you give a reason, too: 'I said I'd finish this report by Thursday'. Be pleasant and firm about it, and stick to your guns once you have made your decision.

Use your out-of-office system wisely

If you are part time, make it a priority to leave up-to-date, out-of-office messages on your answerphone and set up out-of-office replies on your e-mail system for the days you're not in. This will help your colleagues and other work contacts to remember which days you work, and stop people thinking that you are never in. Only give your colleagues your out-of-work contact details if you think it will make life easier for *you*.

Think professional

Some mums can regularly be heard coo-ing down the phone to their little cherub and chatting to all and sundry about the latest cute thing she's done. This is absolutely fine if it fits in with the culture of your workplace, but if you work in a highly pressurised or predominantly male environment, the sad fact is that you risk being seen as unprofessional, even if this is not the case.

'When I'm at work, I just put my work head on and get stuck in. That way I get a proper break from the kids and I appreciate them all the more when I pick them up at the end of the day.'

Judy, GP practice manager and mum to Bethan, four, and Lily, 11 months

Build support for yourself

Being a working mum can sometimes be a lonely experience, especially if there are only a few parents at your place of work or most of the other mums you know aren't working. Building support around you will not only sustain you when you go through difficult times, it will also open up new opportunities and give you a clearer sense of your rights at work.

- **Get online:** lots of parenting websites, including www.mumsnet.com and www.babycentre.co.uk, have discussion boards where working mums can let off steam about work and childcare.

- **Join a formal network:** there are plenty for working parents and working women. Organisations such as Working Families, Prowess and the Women Returners Network are a mine of information on everything from childcare to flexible working, and can be a great way to meet other working mums, too.

- **Seek out a relevant professional organisation:** some work sectors have organisations specifically for working women, such as the Women's Engineering Society. General trade organisations and professional associations, such as the Law Society or the Chartered Institute of Marketing, although not geared specifically towards women, can also offer valuable support and training opportunities.

- **Stay in touch with your health visitor and GP:** make the time to do this as they can help with issues like stress, tiredness, keeping up breastfeeding and so on.

- **Use complementary therapies:** as well as helping to tackle minor health problems, complementary therapies like aromatherapy and reflexology can provide an oasis of relaxation in your busy working week.

- **Set up a working parents' group:** if you know other parents at work, why not set up a group that meets regularly. If there are particular issues that need tackling, such as discrimination or lack of facilities for expressing, you'll be able to present a united front rather than taking it on alone. Alternatively, set up a mums' e-mail group so that you can swap gossip, tips and advice.

● **Set up a working mums' club:** if you know other working mums who live near you, why not set up a dinner or weekend lunch club? This will give you an opportunity to share advice and information, plus a welcome break from your work and home routines.

> *'I'm lucky enough to work from home and each month I meet up with other parents who work from home for a nice lunch. It helps you feel you're not alone and you pick up useful tips, too.'*
>
> Becky, interior designer and mum to Florence, eight, and Lily, five

Succeeding at work

Being a mum and pursuing a high-octane career at the same time requires a huge amount of commitment, drive and energy. It certainly isn't for everyone, and many working mums are content to slip into a lower gear for a while. However, other working mums complain that, once they return to work, the decision to downgrade their career is made for them. Many feel undervalued, underpaid and overlooked for both training and promotion, particularly if they work part time.

If you feel you are in danger of being sidelined at work, look at some of the following options.

● **Have a plan:** knowing where you are going will help you work towards a happier working life. Sit down with a piece of paper and think about where you'd like to be in three years' time. Then write down the steps you need to take in order for that to happen – is it training you need, more flexible hours, more childcare or a complete change of direction? Decide which step you need to take first, then put it into action.

- **Make the most of being part time:** 40 per cent of mothers work part time compared with just 4 per cent of dads, according to the Women Returners Network. The great thing about part-time work is that it allows you plenty of time to spend with your children. On the downside, people who work part time tend to get less pay, less training and fewer promotions than their full-time colleagues. The government recommends that employers consider part-time staff for promotion in the same way as full-time staff, so do put yourself forward when jobs come up. If nothing else, it will give your employer the message that you are keen to further yourself. Don't be deterred from requesting a pay rise, either, if you feel you have earned it. Part-timers are legally entitled to the same pay and benefits (pro-rata) as their full-time colleagues, so make sure you are not being left behind.

- **Get trained:** working mums can get overlooked for training, particularly when they are part time. This is partly because employers prefer to spend money on training full-time staff who, they assume, will progress more rapidly in their careers. It's also because part-time workers have less access to courses because of their restricted hours. If you feel you are missing out, make sure you keep an eye on upcoming training opportunities, and put yourself forward for them. Speak to your manager about rearranging your days if necessary. Alternatively, organise your own training, either through a local college or through any trade or professional organisations you may belong to.

- **Consider a job-share:** the advantage of a job-share over part-time work is that you are actually fulfilling a full-time role, albeit with a partner. Employers sometimes shy away from job-shares as they use up more resources: two desks to provide, two people to train and so on. However, job-shares also have huge benefits for employers, including better retention of staff, more continuity when one worker is sick or on leave, and less absenteeism. For the job-sharers themselves it means more chance of getting a job at the right level for you, a higher pro-rata income, better career progression and, last but not least, plenty of time to spend with your children. Lots of job adverts now say whether the role is considered suitable for a job-share, but even if this option is not mentioned, it's still worth enquiring.

● **Create change:** if it's the non-family-friendly practices in your workplace that are holding you back, look at trying to get them changed (see page 63).

Summary of Chapter 13

* Use your commuting time and lunch hour to do things you aren't able to do at home, such as reading the paper and studying.
* Try to put baby matters aside while you are at work.
* Make the most of your time at work by managing your time efficiently.
* Learning to communicate effectively with colleagues will help to make your working life easier.
* Build support networks that will sustain you through difficult patches.
* Make sure you don't miss out on training, pay rises and promotions.

CHAPTER 14

The School Years: What You Need to Know

Once your child starts school, emotionally and financially work becomes a lot easier. If you've struggled with feelings of guilt, for example, you'll immediately feel a cloud lifting. After all, while your child is at school, it makes no difference to her if you are at work or not. At the same time, your bank balance will start to feel the difference, too. If you've been working since your child was little, you'll be used to childcare taking a big slice of your income – and now that hard-earned money is yours. If you've been waiting for your child to start school before going back to work, you'll be thrilled to be earning a salary again.

You will, of course, have to think about new issues like after-school care, school holidays and a host of other demands related to school life – like finding time to help with homework and how to schedule the school concert and parents' evenings into your diary. But many of your work skills – negotiating, delegating, motivating – can be put to great advantage at home, too. Getting your child involved in the chores, for example, will not only help you but is also a great way to encourage her independence and boost her self-esteem. Coming to a mutually acceptable agreement about when and where homework should be done will help her to keep on top of her work and avoid unnecessary conflict.

Above all, finding ways to keep life running smoothly will give you the time you want to spend with your child. These are, after all, the golden years – when your child's growing individuality and infectious enthusiasm make being a mum more fun than it's ever been.

The day-to day detail

Being organised and getting into a good routine is the best way to stay on top of the day-to-day detail of your child's life and avoid those classic moments of intense stress (like getting half way down the road only to have to run back because your child has forgotten her lunch box – again).

- **Establish a routine:** and try to keep to it. Setting times for getting up, doing homework and going to bed, for example, will help your child be more co-operative. Getting school bags, clothes and breakfast ready the night before can help keep the mornings as relaxed as possible.

- **Make the timetable visible:** stick your child's school timetable somewhere easy to read (on the fridge or by the front door) so you and she can make sure she has what she needs each day.

- **Make your child responsible:** allocate a box or a peg for the school bag, school PE kit, school shoes, school coat. Every day remind your child to put these away in the right place until she can do this without thinking.

- **Keep a slush fund:** for example, regularly empty your purse of loose change and keep it in a jam jar in the kitchen ready for you to dip into when you need cash for school trips, school dinners and so on.

- **Double up on school uniform:** this is invaluable when items of clothing go missing (under the bed, in the wash, at school!).

- **Get your child involved in chores:** whether it's laying the table, dusting her bedroom, or putting her laundered clothes away – every little bit helps you, and encourages her to be independent. Have a family reward at the end of the week – a film and a big bag of popcorn, for example.

- **Encourage tidy habits:** a great trick is to have a 'lost' property box into which you put anything that's left lying around – socks, parts of toys, pens and pencils – and let your child know that anything that isn't reclaimed by the end of the week will go to a charity shop.

● **Plan ahead:** or at least do so whenever you can. Building in time to deal with big events, like your child's birthday party, will help prevent a build-up of stress.

● **Keep a stock of non-gender-specific party presents:** you'll be amazed how many parties your child gets invited to and having to get to the shops to buy presents can take up lots of time. Instead, buy gifts whenever you see something appropriate and keep them stashed away somewhere safe (with supplies of wrapping paper, cards and sticky tape).

An overview: your healthy, happy child

While the day-to-day detail is important, try not to get too caught up in just keeping life ticking over. It's vital to have an overview of your child's life, too. Of course, getting through each day and doing well at school is important, but so is being healthy and happy. Is she, for example, getting enough exercise? Growing children need to have at least one hour's exercise a day to maintain the right level of fitness. Bear this in mind when you are planning after-school activities or choosing between getting on top of the washing when you get back home or taking your child to the park for a run around.

And there's food. As your child gets older and more independent (away for teas, sleepovers, parties), keeping her from what you might consider 'unhealthy' foods can get harder. And while finding time to sit down and eat as a family can be difficult when you all have different schedules, sitting round the table together, enthusing about 'real' food and dishing the dirt on junk food, is one of the best ways of reinforcing the message about healthy eating.

Your growing child also needs time to play. With hectic schedules (yours and hers) and easy distractions (like television and computer games), opportunities for children to discover the pleasures of play can become few and far between. Trying not to over-schedule your child's life with 'educational' activities, and giving her the time and space to get bored will not only help her discover how to be resourceful and amuse herself but also help her find out more about her interests and talents.

Supporting your child at school

Choosing a school – and for reception-aged children, settling them in – may involve you taking some time off work. So the year your child is due to start formal education (the academic year in which she turns five) you will need to plan your annual leave carefully.

When it comes to deciding which school to send your child to, practical considerations, such as distance from home, for example, will be important. Try to look ahead – you may be able to walk with or drive your child to school now, but will this always be the case? At some point – and certainly by the time she reaches secondary-school age – your child will want to get herself to school. Being able to walk or take a bus will be a huge bonus for both of you. Breakfast and after-school or homework clubs may also be important if you have late and/or early work hours (see page 137).

If you are happy with the standard of food at your child's school, opt for school lunches rather than packed – it's one less thing you have to think about! If you are worried she's not eating enough, make sure she has a good breakfast – porridge, a boiled egg, banana on toast – to keep her going for most of the day. If you have older children, they could be encouraged to make their own sandwiches if they prefer not to have school dinners.

Once they are safely at school, keeping up to speed with what's happening in your child's life can be tricky. Just finding out what they had for lunch may be a struggle as many children don't want to talk about their day once they get home. And if you are not at the school gate to pick up snippets of information from other parents, or have a quick chat with your child's teacher, it's easy to feel out of touch.

So how can you stay up to date with your child's school life – and show that you support and value her education – without giving her the third degree at the end of every day?

Keeping in touch

Your child's life at school needn't be a mystery.

- **Have a place for school paperwork:** this could be a tray or file. Encourage your child to put letters straight into it when she gets home.

- **Plan for parents' evenings:** get the dates for parents' evenings as soon as they are available and schedule them into your work diary. Schools will generally see parents through the afternoon and into the evening and they want you to be involved – so if for some reason it's impossible to make the date on offer, your child's teacher will be happy to see you another time.

- **Think about how you are involved:** be canny about how you get involved in school life. The PTA will always want parents to make cakes and help out at the school fete, but if all you can spare is the occasional afternoon, opt for a high-profile presence – like going into the classroom to help with reading, or accompanying your child on a school trip – which your child will appreciate much more.

- **Encourage school talk:** use open-ended questions like 'What did you have for lunch today?', 'What did the art teacher think of your homework?', 'What was assembly about today?'.

- **Use the school's website:** this is a quick and easy way of keeping up to date with what's going on.

- **Invite your child's friends round:** try to have friends round for tea or a play whenever you can – invariably children end up talking about school when they are all together. You'll also get the chance to meet their friends' parents. If weekday teas are impossible, use the occasional weekend afternoon.

- **Welcome your child's friends and their parents:** once your child is at secondary school, there are naturally fewer opportunities to meet other parents, chat to teachers and generally keep in touch. Welcoming her friends (even those you may not be so keen on!) to your house will help. You could also organise the occasional get-together (a drink or takeaway) with the parents of her friends.

> *'I'm really glad we opted for the local secondary school for Eleanor. I already know some other mums with children at the same school and they help fill in the gaps. Plus I get to know her friends as they live close by.'*
>
> Annabel, GP and mum to Eleanor, 13

Homework

Your child is likely to have homework from an early age. Encouraging good homework habits from the outset will prevent nagging and help her do her best at school.

- **Establish a set time for homework:** agree a time with your child, for example after tea but before television or using the computer. If you can, make it a time when you will be at home as this can make all the difference. She can then talk to you about what she's doing, you can keep in touch with her schoolwork, and she'll feel supported and cared for.

- **Work with your child:** if you have to catch up on office work, do it while your child does her homework – working alongside her will provide great moral support!

- **Avoid arguments:** don't let arguments about homework spoil the evening or weekend. If your child can't manage the homework, write a note to her teacher so she can get the extra support she needs. If you don't feel she's making enough effort, make an appointment with her teacher and take your child with you to discuss the problem.

- **Encourage your child to be organised:** especially once she's at secondary school. Give her a space to keep all her books, and help her get into the habit of checking her homework diary, printing off essays and getting her bag ready the night before.

● **Use examples of your own work:** these can help your child to solve homework problems that involve, for example, research and/or presentation skills.

> '*My husband is in charge of Sunday mornings – he helps the children do their homework, and gets them to their activities. This has really helped him form a good relationship with them.*'
>
> Jackie, school nurse and mum to Eve, 11, and Peter, seven

Term-time and holiday childcare

You will probably have to reassess your arrangements for childcare once your child goes to school. There are various options available, including before- and after-school clubs, childminders and friends.

Before and after school

If you want to continue with your existing childminder, you'll probably find she's very happy to renegotiate your contract so that her responsibilities include dropping your child off at school and/or picking her up at the end of the day and looking after her until you get back from work.

If you are starting afresh – perhaps because you are returning to work after a break, or your childminder can't get to your child's school – you'll need to find a new childminder. Start looking well in advance of the start of the school term so your child can spend some time getting to know her or him. Besides the usual checks (see page 139) you should also establish with the childminder whether your child will be able to do what she wants when she gets back – such as relaxing in front of the television, or getting some homework done. It may also be important that there are other children there of her own age – and not just babies and toddlers.

Breakfast and after-school clubs are another option. Your local Childcare (or Children's) Information Service will tell you what's available in your area – see your local government website for details. They are usually based on the school premises, or at youth or community centres. And even if your child's own school doesn't offer these facilities, the nearest club may well have staff who can drop off or collect your child from their school. Breakfast clubs are usually open from 8am, and after-school clubs usually close between 5.30pm and 6pm. The clubs do cost but there will be other children there the same age, and there will be activities as well as quiet spaces. Breakfast clubs cost from 50p to £1 a day. After-school clubs cost from £3 to £10 a day.

If you work part time, a friend with a child at the same school may be happy to have another child home for tea once or twice a week as a playmate – especially if you can reciprocate every now and again. Bear in mind, however, that this arrangement could become tricky if the children fall out or if your friend wants to change the arrangement to fit in with other commitments like after-school activities.

'I have a long commute so I have to drop the children off early at their breakfast club. But they're fine about this – they get to eat cereal they wouldn't have at home!'

Madeleine, tax officer and mum to Simon, eight, and Claudine, 11

School holidays

Finding care for your child during the school holidays can be difficult so it makes sense to plan well ahead. You and your partner may decide to take some annual leave – either separately or together – so you will probably be looking for a variety of solutions to tide your child over until term starts again.

Lots of parents get through holidays by calling on relatives. Even if they don't live close by, going to stay with grandparents or cousins could be a real treat for your child.

Some after-school clubs also run play schemes during the school holidays but bear in mind that there is usually huge demand for places. You may well need to make yourself available on the first day that bookings are taken to make sure you don't miss out!

Some local authorities and private organisations offer special holiday courses in sports and other activities like music and drama. And day and summer camps – already the norm in America – are becoming increasingly popular over here.

These could be fun for your child – especially if she has a friend to go with – but if you work full time you may still need to find care for before and after the course. You may be able to change your hours during this period to fit in, or find a friend who can drop off and pick up for you.

Choosing a breakfast club, after-school club or holiday scheme or camp

What else do you need to know to reassure yourself that your children will be safe and well cared for?

If the club or scheme is caring for children eight years of age and under for more than two hours a day, the providers can be registered with Ofsted and inspected each year. You can examine the details of an inspection on the Ofsted website (www.ofsted.gov.uk/reports).

In all cases, however, you should take time to check out the club to reassure yourself that your child will be safe and happy while she's there. When you visit, take her with you so you can see how the staff welcome her and interact with her. Choose a time when there are other children there so you see whether they are calm, happy and busy. While you are there, check on the following.

- All clubs and schemes should have a child protection policy.

- All staff and volunteers should have been through a thorough recruitment process including interviews, references and police checks. They should also have had training in child protection and health and safety.

- You may also want to ask about staff qualifications and experience. What do they enjoy about being with children, and how well do they interact with the children?

- All clubs and schemes should have a written code of behaviour outlining good practice on issues such as bullying, shouting, racism and sexism.

- Are the premises clean and safe? Is there a first aid box? Have the premises passed fire regulations?

- Is there plenty of space for your child to play and explore? Is there a warm and welcoming atmosphere?

- What activities are on offer? Are these planned each day, and supported with good resources, toys and equipment?

- Will there be activities that involve going out and about? You should be asked for your consent for any trips – no matter how long or how short.

SUMMARY OF CHAPTER 14

- Organisation is the key to staying on top of the day-to-day detail of your child's life.
- Encouraging healthy habits – like exercise and eating well – are important at this age.
- Keep in touch with your child's school life by getting involved with school events whenever you can, inviting her friends over and even meeting up with her friends' parents.
- Get your child into good homework habits from the outset – it will help avoid conflict when she's older.
- You may want to reassess your childcare: breakfast and after-school clubs offer good wrap-around care during term time. Holiday schemes and camps may be available for school holidays.
- As with any childcare, follow all the usual checks to make sure your child will be safe and happy.

CHAPTER 15

Loving Your Child: Staying Close

It's inevitable when you are at work that you'll fret about not being there for your child, and worry about missing important events like that first step or first sports day. This is hard, but you also know that what really counts for your child is that he is loved and well cared for.

Sometimes, however, as you rush from work to home, to clubs, to tea and to bed, it's easy to find that while you are focusing brilliantly on your child's practical needs, you are not necessarily meeting his emotional needs. After all, children can't read minds, and conveying love isn't just about saying 'I love you'. Love is also expressed in the way you communicate with them, the way you value their company, and the way you accept them. And when the time you have with your child is extra precious because there never seems enough of it, it's even more important to get the loving right.

> 'When my daughter was 14, I found loving her very hard. She wound me up. I'd get irritable and jump down her throat. I knew things could only get worse if I didn't sort them out. I tried to find things we could do together – we started having a regular night out at the cinema. And I looked for the good things she did – just praising her made me feel better, and made it easier for me to feel loving.'
>
> Dynia, charity fundraiser and mum to Tia, 15

Accepting your child for who he is

Unconditional love means accepting your child for who he is. And this means letting go of your own hopes and dreams and letting him find his own. It means not preaching a philosophy of perfection. And it means allowing him to have his own likes and dislikes, even when they are at odds with your own. This shows that you love your child no matter what, and while he knows that there will always be a price to pay for behaving badly, he also knows that the price won't be your love.

Making your child feel special

Whether it's reading a book together, pitting your wits against him on a computer game, or having a regular Saturday morning café treat, doing something together tells your child how much you enjoy his company. Even when you are manically multitasking, taking the phone off the hook, leaving the washing aside and forgetting about work for a moment to sit down with your child ('It's been a busy day, come and sit down with me for a few moments') will make him feel special and loved.

Of course, there will be times when your child makes demands that you can't meet because you are not in the mood or you are too tired. Then it's fine to reschedule: 'I'd love to play the game with you – let's do it after tea.' There may also be times when your child is particularly needy and you can't suggest an alternative. Seeing this as a short-term problem will help you to cope.

Being affectionate

For babies, close physical contact, whether it's cuddling, stroking, kissing or rocking, is incredibly important. Your loving touch helps him feel safe and secure, calms him when he's fretful and helps to develop a close and trusting bond between you both. If you feel he's always being rushed from cot to buggy to car seat and back again, try to make bath time and bedtime special. Massaging your baby will also help him feel close to you. As your child becomes more physically independent, hugs and cuddles become a more valuable way of expressing warmth and tenderness. Older children, however, will often only want to hug when they feel like it – so don't feel rejected if he occasionally spurns your advances! Instead, use watching television or reading him a story as an excuse for snuggling up together.

During the teenage years, your child may naturally become more self-conscious, and shy away from physical contact. But while his body language may be saying 'Don't touch me', physical affection is still important for helping your child feel lovable and attractive. A warm hand on the back and a quick kiss at bedtime will probably be secretly appreciated.

Setting limits and boundaries

It's easy – especially if you feel guilty about working – to fall into the trap of thinking that, by giving him what he wants, you are proving your love for him. But being indulgent and giving into your child's wishes, especially when they are unreasonable or inappropriate, can lead to confusion. Saying 'Yes, you can do what you like' is another way of saying 'I don't care'.

Being prepared instead to say 'no' gives your child clear boundaries and helps him feel safe and supported. As long as he is allowed reasonable freedom within those limits ('No you can't get down until you've eaten some vegetables, but you can choose which you prefer' or 'No you can't stay up tonight and watch the film, but you can stay up later at the weekend'), he will be reassured that you love him and have his best interests at heart.

Giving praise

Noticing when your child does something good – and praising him for it – takes no time, yet is one of the most loving things you can do. And it doesn't have to be something earth shattering like passing a music exam or scoring a goal in the football match. In fact, the things you choose to praise your child for will say a lot about what you value in him – showing your approval when he's kind to his younger brother or when he tries really hard at something he finds difficult. Positive words can make a huge difference in building your child's self-esteem and proving to him that you think he's special.

Being a good listener

One of the best ways to communicate your love to your child is to listen to him. Attentive listening – giving your child your full attention, and letting him speak without interrupting or judging – shows your child you respect him. It makes him feel confident that his opinions, interests and thoughts are worth listening to. It encourages him to open up and communicate with you. And it is also one of the best ways of keeping in touch with your child and how he is developing, especially as he goes through the teenage years, when you are likely to be surprised by some of the changes taking place.

- **Show that you are interested:** when he talks, make eye contact (with smaller children this may mean getting down to their height).

- **Be open:** don't cross your arms or hunch forward in an aggressive or defensive way. If your child feels judged, he'll clam up even before he's started.

- **Let him finish:** don't interrupt with your views or interpretations until he's had his say; if he dries up, just ask a few open questions (What? Why? How?) to encourage him to carry on.

- **Reflect back what you hear:** you can do this by repeating some of the words or phrases or the last sentence your child used, or by commenting on his emotional reactions – for example, 'You seem angry', to show that you understand what he is telling you.

- **Be unshockable:** children often say things for effect or to test your reactions, and shrieking in horror may make him clam up completely.

Communicating honestly

Open, honest communication helps your child to feel supported, understood and close to you. Children should be able to talk freely about what's bothering them, and about what makes them happy.

- **Discuss everyday decisions with your child:** whether it's choosing what to have for supper, which film to rent or where to go on holiday. Inviting your child to contribute his ideas, even when they can't be accommodated, will help him realise how important they are.

- **Create opportunities for talking together:** this is often easier with younger children as they naturally spend more time with you. As older children get more independent you may need to work harder to find opportunities, such as in the car or during family mealtimes.

- **Always try to answer your child's questions:** sometimes these will be easy ('Why do babies cry?'); sometimes more difficult ('Why do you always sound grumpy when Granny phones?'). But sharing with your child an answer that is appropriate for his age and understanding will help him understand the world, understand you and feel safe expressing his thoughts and ideas.

- **Avoid preaching:** if your child has asked a question, or you want to tell him something, it's important to share your point of view and the reasoning behind it without delivering a lecture. Preaching is simply telling a child what to do without explaining why.

SUMMARY OF CHAPTER 15

Children need to be reassured that you love them – and not just with words. When you are spending precious time with your child, you can communicate your love in a number of ways.

- Accept your child for who he is.
- Make your child feel special.
- Be physically affectionate.
- Use positive body language.
- Set limits and boundaries.
- Give praise.
- Be a good listener.
- Communicate openly.

CHAPTER 16

The Teenage Years: What You Need to Know

As your child becomes a teenager your life as a working mum should, in theory, change for the better. You are no longer tied to the school-run, your teen has her own keys to the house and a phone to help her stay in touch, she can get herself from A to B, make simple meals and snacks for herself and, hopefully, keep on top of her school or college work and her other responsibilities.

In practice, your teenager's new-found freedom may also raise new fears and worries for you. Sure, it's great that your child can get herself to and from school, but you might be worried that once school's over she just slumps in front of the computer until you get back, or cries because she's had a bad day and there's no one at home to talk to, or perhaps doesn't even come home – but sits in the park with her friends, drinking, smoking or worse!

Of course, all these things could happen, but if you have a strong and loving relationship with your child, and make sure she has the skills and knowledge she needs to take care of herself and act responsibly, even when you are not around, chances are both she and you will get through this period unscathed.

The key is to use the time you have with her carefully. Handling her with sensitivity, maintaining reasonable limits and boundaries, boosting her confidence and, as always, giving unconditional affection will all help her stay on an even keel.

'I think on the whole my children have benefited from me working. They are very supportive, and have a good attitude to work themselves.'

Anne, educational psychologist and mum to Ellen, 16, and Ross, 14

Learning to care for herself

As a working mum you are not going to be on hand every moment of the day to keep a watchful eye over your teen, but she's not too young to learn how to care for herself – and encouraging her to think about her own personal well-being and safety now will help her establish good habits that will last a lifetime. Helping her see the benefits of staying fit and healthy will help her cope with the huge physical and emotional changes that come with puberty, as will taking the time to make sure she has all the information she needs to keep herself safe.

'I use TV programmes – especially the soaps – to discuss issues like drugs or unwanted pregnancies. My daughter seems to find it easier to understand the consequences when she can relate to a TV character!'

Ruth, catering assistant and mum to Stephanie, 15, and Owen, ten

Staying fit and healthy

- **Food:** don't be surprised if you are always coming home to find she's raided the fridge – your teen is growing fast and needs extra calories to keep up her energy levels. Stock up with healthy snacks so she doesn't resort to crisps, biscuits and fizzy drinks – and show her where you keep the shopping list so she can add to it when she finishes the last of the crackers!

- **Exercise:** encourage her to take up active after-school clubs. Not only will this give her something to do during those hours when you are not around, but being active will also boost her health and her moods. Motivate her into action by explaining the feel-good factor of being active.

● **Sleep:** make sure she's getting enough of it. She ought to be having at least nine hours a night – deep sleep is vital to help her grow and develop properly.

Staying safe

As your teenager becomes more independent she'll also become more exposed to potential dangers. Making sure she's properly informed about the risks she might face will help keep her safe.

● **Out and about:** establish ground rules for when your teenager is out with friends. These might include always telling you where she's going (remind her that even when you are stuck in a meeting she can leave a message), and keeping you informed if she changes her plans; not being a passenger if the driver has been drinking (or driving herself if she's been drinking); getting home at the agreed time or risking a loss of privileges. Talking to her about personal safety is important, too – for example, not walking home late at night on her own, choosing a busy carriage to travel in on the train and so on.

● **Sex:** research shows that your teenager is more likely to wait to have sex for the first time, and be more savvy about protection against sexually transmitted diseases and unwanted pregnancy, if she is properly informed. And studies also show the person she most wants to hear it from is you. Look for appropriate moments to talk about the subject, in a relaxed and open way, rather than just having one major discussion, as there is a lot of information to take in. Make sure she understands the mechanics and risks of sex. Talk about contraception – and how condoms are the only way to protect against common sexually transmitted diseases such as chlamydia (which is especially prevalent among teenagers).

- **Alcohol, drugs and smoking:** try to avoid lecturing your child about these issues – instead, make the point that your main concern is her health, safety and well-being. Take the time also to gen up on the subject – schools provide lots of information on drugs, for example – and check that your teenager properly understands it, too, including the risks and dangers, and how the law stands. As with all types of peer pressure, being able to say no depends to a huge extent on your child feeling secure in herself (see Boosting your child's confidence, page 152).

School and school holidays

By this age, your child will be expected by her school to motivate herself. But there's still lots you can do to help her get organised and stay engaged.

- **Keep in touch:** work commitments might mean you can't always be at home when she gets back, but a text, e-mail or even a good old-fashioned phone call can reassure her that you are thinking of her.

- **Be there:** being on hand when your child is doing her homework can make a real difference. Help her plan her after-school routine so you can be there as often as possible.

- **Provide somewhere quiet to work:** if the computer is more interesting to her than her work, move it into a family room so you can keep a watchful eye on how much time she's spending in front of the screen.

- **Be involved:** get clued up on her subjects, coursework, school expectations and so on. For example, you don't need to become an expert in Shakespeare, but reading one of her set texts might be fun and give you a point of contact. And the more you know about her school life, the more interest you can show.

- **Plan ahead:** parents' evenings, curriculum evenings and other school meetings and events are often scheduled in advance by the school – put the dates into your diary as soon as possible so you can juggle work events accordingly.

- **Use an in-tray:** have a box or folder in the kitchen for your child to put school letters into as soon as she gets home. Then you can deal with them in your own time rather than have your child demand you fill in a form and produce the money for a school trip just as you are dashing off to catch a train.

- **Use a family calendar:** encourage your child to look at it and think ahead so she can plan homework around family events and her other activities.

- **Be organised:** allocate a shelf for your child's school books, and make sure she has enough files and dividers for organising each subject.

- **Be there at exam time:** keep some of your annual leave available to use during your child's exams. Being on hand to offer supportive cups of tea and delicious snacks during revision, checking that she's not getting overwrought (or 'underwrought'!), diverting panicky calls from her friends, and helping test her if she asks – this can make all the difference to your child and her ability to cope successfully at this time.

- **Plan for holiday times:** keep your teenager busy during the holidays – get her to sign up for courses, or find herself a temporary job. And establish house rules for when you are not around – for example, she must check with you before inviting friends over.

'I took a week off when Tom did his GCSEs – just being around to check the times of his exams and make sure he got to school on time helped him cope better.'

Bea, pharmaceutical marketing manager and mum to Tom, 16, and Roy, 14

Boosting your child's confidence

As a working mum you are already providing a strong, confident and capable role model for your children. You can keep up the good work at home, too, by taking every opportunity you can to boost your child's confidence. Good self-esteem will help your teenager be less dependent on her peer group for approval, and make it easier to resist the pressure to do things she's not sure about. Her confidence will also help you feel better about her ability to care for herself.

- **Don't do everything for her:** don't compensate for going out to work by doing everything for her – or making all her decisions. This doesn't mean you can't guide her with advice and suggestions, but getting her to do things herself and think what's best for her will give her a strong sense of self-worth.

- **Listen to her opinions and ideas:** even if you don't agree with her, taking her thoughts seriously will make her feel that she's valued.

- **Try not to argue:** when you have a dispute, give her the chance to say her bit before saying yours. Two-way communication rather than an 'I'm right, you're wrong' row will help her feel that she's being taken seriously.

- **Try to praise more often than you criticise:** she might drive you mad for not keeping her room tidy, leaving the milk out or forgetting her lunch box, but a few positive comments will make it easier for her to take on board the negative ones ('Thanks for taking out the rubbish – I'm really pushed for time today. Can you tidy up your clothes now, too?').

- **Find opportunities to treat her like an adult:** get her to book tickets for the cinema, or make a shopping list for the supermarket run.

- **Don't be afraid to say no:** the biggest temptation for working mums is to avoid conflict by giving in to moods. Even though she may rage against you, setting boundaries and limits shows that you care, and makes her feel secure. And the more loved and valued she feels at home, the more confidence she'll have in the outside world.

> *'My son and I used to have a lot of arguments because he's so untidy. Now I've given him clear guidelines and explained why all of us have a responsibility to keep our shared family space clean and tidy. His bedroom is still a bit of a mess, but at least now he clears up after himself in the kitchen.'*
>
> Jenine, loss adjuster and mum to Conor, 15

Staying close

Keeping in touch with children's thoughts, fears, hopes and dreams becomes harder when they are teenagers. Your teen is naturally spending more time away from you, and when you are working, too, you may feel that your paths rarely cross. When you are in the same house, or car, or café together, you need to make the time count. This doesn't mean pinning your teen down and giving her the third degree, but making conversation, giving off friendly vibes and generally trying to enjoy each other's company. Here are some suggestions on how to make the relationship work.

- **Be there at key times:** try to be around as often as possible for key times like breakfast, after school, supper and bedtime. Family meals are especially important as everyone automatically talks about their day.

- **Reschedule other activities:** if you find that activities like a fitness class or book club are keeping you out of the house when your teenager is usually around, see if you can reschedule.

- **Make a supper date:** try to have one evening a week when the whole family is together for supper. Make the meal an event – even if you just order a takeaway you can still get out the candles.

- **Recognise her need for privacy:** from knocking on her bedroom door before you go in, to not expecting her to share her every thought with you. Allowing her privacy shows that you respect her as an individual.

- **Be available to talk to:** regularly reassure her that if she's worried about something or just wants to talk, you will always be there for her. Don't grill her, but make sure that you have quiet times together when she can open up to you if she feels like it, for example when you are shopping together, in the car or over a meal.

- **Keep in touch with other parents:** if you regularly bump into her friends' mums when picking up from sleepovers and parties, why not suggest a get-together? This is a great way to keep in touch with your teenager's life, and pick up useful info about school and other activities.

> *'I'd love to be at home for when my children get in from school, but usually I'm not in until around sixish. On the upside, because they are alone together quite a lot, they've developed a really good relationship.'*
>
> Susan, communications manager and mum to Tessa, 17, and Allison, 15

- **Don't be overprotective:** your teenager needs to make mistakes, big and small, to learn, even if this means walking home in the rain because she's forgotten her bus fare, or failing an exam because she hasn't worked hard enough.

- **Be a good listener:** when she does talk to you, stop or slow down what you are doing and give her your full attention (a common complaint from teenagers is that their parents never really listen).

- **Think before you speak:** choose your words carefully and don't be judgemental or angry. She's less likely to open up to you again if you over-react. Instead, focus on exploring ways to deal with the problem.

- **Tell her that you love her:** she may not always be approachable, and she may well prefer to spend most of her time with her friends, but you are still her rock, and reassuring her that you care will help her feel confident about turning to you when she needs help and support.

SUMMARY OF CHAPTER 16

As your child becomes a teenager, in many ways your life as a working mum gets easier.

- Feel confident that your teen can be trusted when you are not around by ensuring she knows how to care for herself and stay fit, healthy and safe.
- Help her stay motivated at school by encouraging good homework habits, keeping clued up about her school life and being available to help during exams.
- A lack of confidence will affect her self-esteem and make it harder for her to resist negative peer pressure. Find ways to boost her confidence and help her feel good about herself.
- Stay close by keeping lines of communication open.

CHAPTER 17

Family Well-being: How to Get Along

Family life will always have its ups and downs. However much you care about your partner and love and enjoy your children, there will be good days (laughter, companionship, warmth) and bad (arguments, moods and tension).

When you work, time at home is especially precious and you don't want to spend your weekends or evenings arguing with your partner or sorting out sibling disagreements. So how can you improve family relationships and create a happy and harmonious home?

Often the mood of the house will be set by you. If you and your partner are grumpy or quarrelling, chances are your children will pick up on the atmosphere and their own behaviour will deteriorate, too. In a household where the parents are generally kind and respectful towards each other, and can deal productively with disagreements, children are more likely to interact with their friends and any brothers or sisters in the same way.

Making your relationship work

Creating a stable and happy relationship isn't always easy. From the moment your baby is born, the dynamics of your relationship will be challenged. Who, for example, do you put first – your children, or your partner? You may discover qualities in each other you never knew existed – some good (tenderness, patience), some bad (one-upmanship, selfishness). Your ideal may have been to work as a team, while in reality one person may end up doing the lion's share.

Keeping your relationship not just intact but buoyant throughout these years involves real commitment.

- **Be generous:** dole out as many doses of generosity as you can. This not only shows how much you love your partner, but also helps you to feel good about yourself.

- **Give yourself lots of praise:** there will be times when you have to be your own cheerleader and you won't always be able to rely on your partner for the feedback you need or deserve. Don't let this come between you. Give yourself a pat on the back instead.

- **Avoid trying to 'win':** relationships have to be partnerships, even if circumstances sometimes mean that they are unequal ones, and competitiveness (always wanting to have the last word, for example), can only ever be destructive.

- **Be assertive:** if you have a problem, talk about it, and be specific. Say 'I was cross when ...' rather than 'You always ...'. Don't imagine just because you look grumpy or act prickly that your partner will know what's up.

- **Make an effort:** with the demands of work and the children, the times you have together may be few and far between. It's easy to get lazy. Think about the energy you put into being fun to be with when you are with your friends, and try to do the same with your partner.

- **Speak to each other as you wish to be spoken to:** squabbling and bickering can become a habit, creating a depressing atmosphere and a way of interacting that will be copied by your children.

- **Keep communicating:** not just about the day-to-day stuff, but about your hopes and dreams, likes and dislikes.

- **Don't let practical issues come between you:** if household tasks are a cause of conflict, agree to bring in outside help.

- **Be realistic:** don't feel guilty about the occasional argument – they are a fact of life. Seeing you resolve them amicably and constructively will help your children learn how to sort out their own difficulties with you, friends and siblings.

> *'Now the children are older, Mike, my husband, and I have more time alone together. Megan babysits once a week so we can pop out for a quick drink or to the pictures.'*
>
> Emma, office administrator and mum to Megan, 14, and Elizabeth, 12

Sibling harmony

If you have two or more children, you will know all about sibling rivalry. It can range from trivial bickering ('Mum, Jack's squashing me', '...eating with his mouth open', '...still in the loo!'), to name calling ('Idiot', 'You're ugly and fat', 'You're both and stupid with it!') and aggression (snatching, hitting, poking, prodding).

When your time with your children is so precious, it's really disheartening to have the mood infected by silly squabbling. Naturally you want your home to feel warm and friendly, a place where you can shine as a loving and caring mother, not a place where you are constantly compelled to referee sibling bickering, and nag your children for not being nicer to each other.

So why do children do it? Often because they are bored – and because it's fun. Often because they believe something is unfair, or they are protecting their territory, or their possession. Sometimes because they feel neglected, and it gets them some attention.

Minor sibling squabbles can be extremely tiresome, but on the whole are unlikely to do any lasting damage. And often they are a good way for children to learn how to compromise, negotiate, forgive and forget. More serious or extreme rivalry, however, may be a sign of emotional instability, and could have a big impact on how your child sees himself, and how he relates to others in adult life. For your own sanity, and to help your children form strong and lasting friendships with each other, it makes sense to try to keep upsets to a minimum and to prevent differences getting out of control.

Reducing rivalry

Keep a check on how you treat each child. There will inevitably be times when one child is easier to manage than another, or is just more compatible with you. Accept this, and rather than aiming to love them equally, think about loving them uniquely. Treating them as individuals, and giving them the love, care and attention that suits their own needs will help them feel special, and less competitive for your attention.

- **Resist labelling:** pigeon-holing one child as 'the clever one', 'the sporty one', 'the co-operative one' or 'the argumentative one' can simply fuel bad feeling between brothers and sisters and become self-fulfilling.

- **Avoid comparisons:** even if you are doing it with the best intentions, for example to boost your child's sense of achievement ('You did so much better than your brother'), your child will feel judged in relation to that sibling, and any sense of rivalry will simply be strengthened.

Dealing with fights and arguments

- **Outlaw physical aggression of any sort:** adopting a policy of zero tolerance when it comes to snatching, hitting, scratching and punching from the earliest age helps put the message across loud and clear.

- **Enforce house rules:** if fighting does occur, remind children of the house rules, and separate them. Tell them both to go to their rooms until they have calmed down.

- **Look for a pattern:** if fights or arguments always happen at the same time of day, or over the same issue, find ways to change the routine to sort out the issue.

- **Don't interfere:** when there are arguments, try not to step in. Unless it looks like it's going to escalate into something physical, it's better to give your children the chance to learn how to settle disputes peacefully.

- **Avoid becoming piggy in the middle:** asking questions like 'Who started it?' or 'Why has this happened?' will simply rope you into the argument, fuel the anger and prolong the fight.

- **If you need to step in:** start by simply describing the problem ('OK, there's only one biscuit left and you both want it') without taking sides or judging. Then tell your children that you are confident they can sort it out, and leave them to it.

> *'My boys will fight over anything – from who has the largest slice of cake to who's best at football, running or ice-skating! But as long as they're not hurting each other, I try to stay out of it.'*
>
> Mumtaz, mum to Khadija, nine, and Andul-Jalil, 11

Having fun

Friends and relatives will tell you time and again 'They grow up so quickly; enjoy them while you can'. And, of course, it's true. Childhood, compared to our total life span, is incredibly short. And when you are working, too, time seems to pass in a flash. So it's vital that throughout their lives you grab all the opportunities you can to have fun together and to build up a bank of happy and warm memories for you all to share.

Weekends

When you are a working mum, it's inevitable that there are some chores that need doing at the weekend, and children may need taking to and from their own activities. But, if you are not careful, it's easy to reach Sunday evening without having spent any time together as a family. As your children get older – and especially when they are teenagers and making their own plans – it's increasingly easy to feel as if you are all just orbiting the house, rarely crossing paths. So how can you make sure you spend time together?

- **Organise family activities:** younger children will naturally demand your attention, and will love it if you allocate part of the day over the weekend to a family activity like going for a swim, a cycle ride, a walk in the woods or a day out at a nearby attraction.

- **Have family meals:** children of all ages love sitting down for a big family meal. Whether it's a cooked breakfast on Saturday morning or a traditional roast lunch on Sunday, make it a regular event. With lots of chatter and good humour, even your more reluctant teenager won't be able to resist joining in.

- **Plan ahead:** try to make a couple of arrangements each month that get put in the family diary. It's all too easy for other people's plans – children's parties, for example – to end up dominating your weekend, but if you have a previous arrangement, it's easier to turn down invitations that don't involve the whole family.

- **Organise regular treats:** watching a family film together on a Friday night, having a drink and a snack in a favourite café on Saturday morning, shopping trips – these can quickly become part of the fabric of family life and last forever in your child's memory as happy family occasions.

Holidays

Children love holidays, and for obvious reasons. You are away from home and work, and all the responsibilities that go with holding down a job and running a house. And this gives you plenty of free time to spend as a family. Sometimes, however, winding down and getting into a holiday mood can take a while, and spending a condensed amount of time together can come as a shock! So how can you make it work?

- **Choose your holiday carefully:** you'll be keen for a rest, and hotels are great if you want to be pampered and aim to take advantage of organised children's activities and crèches, but you may be tied in to mealtimes, and you may feel tense if your children aren't free to run around or laugh and shout. Self-catering gives you more freedom but if you are keen to avoid supermarket runs you'll want there to be pubs and restaurants nearby that are both affordable and child-friendly.

- **Leave work behind:** don't stuff any reports into your suitcase 'for looking at during a quiet moment'. Don't take your laptop with you. Don't even give your office a number where you can be contacted. This is your holiday, it's quite legitimate for you to be out of contact, and if the office can't cope while you are away then that's a problem that needs sorting before you go.

- **Get in the right frame of mind:** if you decide beforehand that you are going to have a good time, even if things go wrong (you get lost, children get grumpy, it rains non-stop) you are more likely to be able to laugh about it and keep the atmosphere happy. Remember your priority is to enjoy each other's company – not get a great sun tan.

- **Relax:** when you are used to rushing about and getting things done, you may find chilling out difficult, but being on holiday isn't about ticking off a list of activities done or sights seen. You will have plenty of time for doing that when the children have left home.

- **Don't expect gratitude:** just because you are on holiday and you have gone to lots of trouble and expense, your children won't suddenly turn into little angels and be on their best behaviour. In fact, holidays can often be unsettling for small children, and even older children need to adjust to a different pace. There will still be all the normal squabbles – they'll just be about different things.

SUMMARY OF CHAPTER 17

- It makes sense to work at your relationship with your partner – the happier you both are, the happier and more harmonious the whole family will be.
- Deal with sibling rivalry by making each child feel special.
- Plan weekends so you have at least some time together as a family.
- Make holidays work by not expecting too much, leaving work behind and concentrating on enjoying each other's company.

Sources of Further Information

Pregnancy and birth

The Active Birth Centre
25 Bickerton Road, London N19 5JT
020 7281 6760
www.activebirthcentre.com
Information and classes on natural active childbirth

ARC (Antenatal Results and Choices)
73 Charlotte Street, London W1T 4PN
020 7631 0285 (10am–5.30pm weekdays)
www.arc-uk.org
Information and support around antenatal testing and when an abnormality is diagnosed

BLISS (Baby Life Support Systems)
2nd & 3rd Floors, 9 Holyrood Street, London Bridge, London SE1 2EL
0500 618 140 (10am–5pm weekdays)
www.bliss.org.uk
Support for parents of premature and special needs babies

Anna McGrail and Daphne Metland
Expecting – Everything You Need to Know About Pregnancy, Labour and Birth, Virago Press, 1-94408-034-X

Miscarriage Association
c/o Clayton Hospital, Northgate, Wakefield, West Yorkshire WF1 3JS
01924 200 799 (9am–4pm weekdays)
www.miscarriageassociation.org.uk
Advice and information on a national network of miscarriage support groups

National Childbirth Trust
Alexandra House, Oldham Terrace, Acton, London W3 6NH
0870 444 8707 (9am–5pm Monday–Thursday, 9am–4pm Friday)
www.nct.org.uk
Antenatal classes and postnatal help

NHS Smoking in Pregnancy Helpline
0800 1690 169
Support to help stop smoking

SANDS (Stillbirth and Neonatal Death Society)
28 Portland Place, London W1B 1LY
020 7436 5881 (9.30am–5.30pm weekdays)
www.uk-sands.org
National support network for bereaved parents

Vegetarian Society
Parkdale, Durham Road, Altrincham, Cheshire WA14 4QG
0161 925 2000 (8.30am–5pm weekdays)
www.vegsoc.org
Information on vegetarian diets during pregnancy and for infants

Working Families
1–3 Berry Street, London EC1V 0AA
0800 013 0313
www.workingfamilies.org.uk
Advice and information for working families and employers

Baby and childcare

Association of Breastfeeding Mothers
PO Box 207, Bridgwater, Somerset TA6 7YT
08444 122 949 (9.30am–10.30pm)
www.abm.me.uk
Information, encouragement and support for breastfeeding mothers, mothers-to-be and their families

Association for Post Natal Illness
145 Dawes Road, London SW6 7EB
020 7386 0868 (10am–2pm Monday, Wednesday, Friday; 10am–5pm Tuesday and Friday)
www.apni.org
Advice for women with postnatal depression

www.bbc.co.uk/parenting
Information and advice on pregnancy, childcare and family matters

BLISS (Baby Life Support Systems)
2nd & 3rd Floors, 9 Holyrood Street, London Bridge, London SE1 2EL
0500 618 140 (10am–5pm weekdays)
www.bliss.org.uk
Support for parents of premature and special needs babies

The Breastfeeding Network
PO Box 11126, Paisley, PA2 8YB
08444 124 664
www.breastfeedingnetwork.org.uk
Support and information for breastfeeding women

Dr Jane Collins (consultant editor)
Baby and Child Health, Dorling Kindersley, 1-4053-0063-9

Dr Carol Cooper (consultant editor)
Johnson's Mother and Baby, Dorling
Kindersley, 9-78-140531469-5

Cry-sis
BM Cry-sis
London WC1N 3XX
08451 228 669 (9am–10pm weekdays)
Support for families with excessively
crying, sleepless and demanding babies

Dorothy Einon
Child Behaviour, Viking, 0-670-85968-0

Family Rights Group
Second Floor, The Print House,
18 Ashwin Street, London E8 3DL
0800 731 1696 (10am–12pm and
1.30–3.30pm weekdays)
www.frg.org.uk
Advice and support for families whose
children are involved with social care
services

Family Welfare Association
501–505 Kingsland Road, London E8 4AU
020 7254 6251
www.fwa.org.uk
Support for poorer families, providing
grants and social work advice

For Parents by Parents
109 High Street, Thame, Oxon OX9 3DZ
01844 210 032
www.forparentsbyparents.com
UK parenting site, funded and
maintained by parents

Gingerbread
307 Borough High Street, London
SE1 1JH
0800 018 5026 (9am–5pm Monday–
Friday, 9am–8pm Wednesday)
www.gingerbread.org.uk
Advice and support for lone-parent
families

Home-Start
2 Salisbury Road, Leicester LE1 7QR
0116 233 9955
www.home-start.org.uk
Emotional and practical support for
families in local communities across
the UK

La Leche League GB
PO Box 29, West Bridgford, Nottingham
NG2 7NP
0845 120 2918 (calls taken by mothers
in their own home)
www.laleche.org.uk
Breastfeeding support from pregnancy
through to weaning

Gael Lindenfield
Confident Teens, Thorsons,
0-00-710062-0

MAMA (Meet A Mum Association)
54 Lillington Road, Radstock BA3 3NR
0845 120 3746 (7–10pm weekdays)
www.mama.co.uk
Advice and support for depressed and
isolated mothers

Mothers Over 40
www.mothersover40.com
Online advice and support for older
mums and dads

National Childbirth Trust
Alexandra House, Oldham Terrace,
Acton, London W3 6NH
0870 444 8707 (9am–5pm Monday–
Thursday, 9am–4pm Friday)
www.nct.org.uk
Antenatal classes and postnatal help

www.netmums.com
A local network for mums and dads

NSPCC
Weston House, 42 Curtain Road, London
EC2A 3NH
0808 800 5000 (help and advice for
adults)
0808 1111 (help for children and young
people)
www.nspcc.org.uk
Parent and family support

Parentline Plus
520 Highgate Studios, 53–79 Highgate
Road, London NW5 ITL
0808 800 2222
www.parentlineplus.org.uk
Support and information for parents

Jan Parker and Jan Stimpson
Sibling Rivalry, Sibling Love, Hodder
Mobius, 0-340-79346-5

Raising Kids
www.raisingkids.co.uk
Information, advice and help for anyone
raising kids

Singleparents UK
www.singleparents.org.uk
Online community for single parents
with information, advice, first-hand
experiences and details of local groups

**TAMBA (Twins and Multiple Births
Association)**
2 The Willows, Gardner Road, Guildford,
Surrey GU1 4PG
0800 138 0509 (10am–1pm and
7pm–10pm)
www.tamba.org.uk
Support and information for families of
twins, triplets and more

Vegetarian Society
Parkdale, Durham Road, Altrincham,
Cheshire WA14 4QG
0161 925 2000 (8.30am–5pm weekdays)
www.vegsoc.org
Information on vegetarian diets during
pregnancy and for infants

Childcare

ChildcareLink
0800 234 6346
www.childcarelink.gov.uk
Government website and helpline that
aims to help people find the right
childcare in their area

Daycare Trust
21 St George's Road, London SE1 6ES
020 7840 3350 (Mondays, Wednesdays
and Fridays 10am–5pm)
www.daycaretrust.org.uk
Advice for parents, carers and employers,
trade unions and policymakers on
childcare issues

**National Childminding Association of
England and Wales**
Royal Court, 81 Tweedy Road, Bromley,
Kent BR1 1TG
0845 880 0044
www.ncma.org.uk
Information for parents in England and
Wales who are considering employing a
childminder

One Parent Families
255 Kentish Town Road, London
NW5 2LX
0800 018 5026 (9am–5pm weekdays)
www.oneparentfamilies.org.uk
Information and advice for lone parents

Hilary Pereira
The Good Childcare Guide,
Prentice Hall Life, 978-0-273-71263-3

Pre-school Learning Alliance
The Fitzpatrick Building, 188 York Way,
London N7 9AD
020 7697 2500
www.pre-school.org.uk
Information about pre-schools

Tax Credit helpline
0845 300 3900 (8am–8pm)
Help with claiming tax credits, including
the Working Tax Credit

Child health and nutrition

Allergy UK
3 White Oak Square, London Road,
Swanley, Kent BR8 7AG
01322 619 898
www.allergyuk.org
Information for people with allergies and
food intolerances

Catherine Atkinson
*The Start Right Baby and Toddler Meal
Plan*, Foulsham, 0-572-02974-8

Joanna Blythman
The Food Our Children Eat, Fourth
Estate,1-857-02936-4

The British Dietetic Association
5th Floor, Charles House, 148–149 Great
Charles Street, Queensway, Birmingham
B3 3HT
0121 200 8080
www.bda.uk.com
Information on the latest food and health
issues

British Nutrition Foundation
High Holborn House, 52–54 High
Holborn, London WC1V 6RQ
020 7404 6504
www.nutrition.org.uk
Healthy-eating information

Child Accident Prevention Trust
22–26 Farringdon Lane, London
EC1R 3HA
020 7608 3828
www.capt.org.uk
Advice on reducing accidental childhood injuries

NHS Direct
0845 46 47 (24 hours a day, seven days a week)
Immediate advice on any concerns you may have about yourself or your baby

Ellen Shanley and Colleen Thompson
Fueling the Teen Machine, Bull Publishing, 0-923-52157-7

Peter Vaughan
Simply Better Food for your Baby and Children, Foulsham, 0-572-03003-7

Relationships

Alan Bradley and Jody Beveridge
How to Help the Children Survive the Divorce, Foulsham, 978-0-572-02956-2

Relate
Premier House, Carolina Court, Lakeside, Doncaster DN4 5RA
0845 456 1310
www.relate.org.uk
Advice, relationship counselling, sex therapy and a range of other relationship support services

OnDivorce
0906 633 0247 (Speak to a specialist lawyer, £1.50 per minute, 9am–9pm)
www.ondivorce.co.uk
Resource for those experiencing divorce

Work

Acas National
Brandon House, 180 Borough High Street, London SE1 1LW
0845 747 4747
Employment advice

www.bbc.co.uk/parenting/work
Information and advice for working parents

Citizens Advice Bureau
www.adviceguide.org.uk
Provides online advice and help to find your local bureau

Community Legal Service
0845 345 4 345 (9am–6.30pm weekdays)
www.clsdirect.org.uk
Legal advice and information on finding a legal adviser with the CLS quality mark in your area

Department for Business Enterprise and Regulatory Reform
www.berr.gov.uk
Publishes *Pregnancy and Work* leaflet for pregnant employees

Equality and Human Rights Commission
Arndale House, Arndale Centre, Manchester M4 3EQ
0845 604 6610 (England)
0845 604 8810 (Wales)
0845 604 5510 (Scotland)
www.equalityhumanrights.com
Information and support for people who have been unfairly treated at work because of their gender

Health and Safety Executive
www.hse.gov.uk
Publishes *A guide for new and expectant mothers who work*

Law Centres Federation
Third Floor, 293–299 Kentish Town Road, London NW5 2TJ
020 7428 4400
www.lawcentres.org.uk
Information on free legal advice centres in your area

Kay Marles, Sarah Litvinoff, Lucy Daniels, Parents at Work, Working Mothers Association
Balancing Work and Home: a practical guide to managing stress, 0-9508792-9-0

Prowess
Lion House, 20–28 Muspole Street, Norwich NR3 1DJ
01603 762355
www.prowess.org.uk
Association of organisations and individuals who support women to start and grow businesses

TIGER (Tailored Interactive Guidance on Employment Rights)
tiger.direct.gov.uk
Interactive government website that helps you work out your maternity rights

Steve Wharton
High-vibrational Thinking: How to Get Back to Work, Foulsham, 978-0-572-03078-0

Steve Wharton
High-vibrational Thinking: How to Restore Your Life–Work Balance, Foulsham, 978-0-572-03077-3

Women Returners Network
www.women-returners.co.uk
Advice and support for women returning to work after taking a break

Working Families
1–3 Berry Street, London EC1V 0AA
0800 013 0313
www.workingfamilies.org.uk
Advice and information for working families and employers

For children and teenagers

beat (beating eating disorders)
103 Prince of Wales Road, Norwich NR1 1DW
0845 634 7650 (youthline 4.30–8.30pm weekdays, 1–4.30pm Saturday)
07786 20 18 20 (textline)
0845 634 1414 (adult helpline 10.30am–8.30pm weekdays, 1–4.30pm Saturday)
www.edauk.com
Information and support regarding eating disorders

Brook Advisory Centre
421 Highgate Studios, 53–79 Highgate Road, London NW5 1TL
0800 018 5023 (9am–5pm weekdays)
www.brook.org.uk
Advice on sex and contraception for young people

Childline
0800 1111
www.childline.org.uk
Free 24-hour helpline for children and young people

Frank
0800 77 66 00 (free, 24 hours a day, seven days a week)
www.talktofrank.com
Confidential drug information and advice

Robie H Harris
Let's Talk About Sex: Growing Up, Changing Bodies, Sex and Sexual Health, Walker Books, 978-1-844-28174-9

Kidscape
2 Grosvenor Gardens, London SW1W 0DH
08451 205 204 (for parents, guardians or concerned relatives and friends of bullied children)
www.kidscape.org.uk
Charity to prevent child abuse and bullying

National Self Harm Network
PO Box 7264, Nottingham NG1 6WJ
www.nshn.co.uk
Support for people who self-harm and their family and friends

Sexwise
0800 28 29 30
www.ruthinking.co.uk
Free, confidential advice

Steve Wharton
High-vibrational Thinking: How to Stop that Bully, Foulsham, 0-572-03075-4

Young Minds
48–50 St John Street, London EC1M 4DG
0800 018 2138 (10am–1pm Monday and Friday, 1pm–4pm Tuesday and Thursday, 1pm–4pm and 6pm–8pm Wednesday)
www.youngminds.org.uk
Mental health support for the young

Index